HEAVEN ON EARTH

IN MARRIAGE & RELATIONSHIPS

Bringing the atmosphere of heaven into your love relationships

EMMANUEL OGBECHIE

Unless otherwise indicated, all Scripture quotations are taken from the *King James Version* of the Bible.

HEAVEN ON EARTH
IN MARRIAGE & RELATIONSHIPS

Bringing the atmosphere of heaven into your love relationships

ISBN: 978-0-639-95691-6

Copyright 2018 by EMMANUEL OGBECHIE

Published by Light Edge Systems Pty

Johannesburg, South Africa

Printed in South Africa. All rights reserved under International Copyright Law. Contents and/or cover may not be reproduced in whole or in part in any form without express written consent of the publisher.

TABLE OF CONTENTS

Introduction..v

Chapter 1   The Atmosphere of Heaven in Marriage & Relationships...1

Chapter 2   Imbibing the Culture and Lifestyle of Heaven............5

Chapter 3   Creating Heaven in your Relationships....................11

Chapter 4   The Law of Respect in Relationships......................19

Chapter 5   The Law of Recognition in Relationships................29

Chapter 6   Preserving Friendship & Magnetism......................39

Chapter 7   Grace Based Love..45

Chapter 8   Bringing the God Kind of Love into Your Relationships..53

Chapter 9   Conflict Resolution..57

Chapter 10   Submission the Kingdom way to a Joyous Marriage...63

Chapter 11   How to Deal with a Difficult Spouse......................69

Chapter 12   Longsuffering in Relationships...............................73

Chapter 13   Communication In Relationship..............................79

Chapter 14   Harvesting Honey from your Honey Producer........91

Chapter 15   What Men & Women want from their Spouses........97

Chapter 16   The Man, Father, Husband & Leader.....................103

Chapter 17   God's Instruction to Husbands...............................117

INTRODUCTION

Therefore shall ye lay up these my words in your heart and in your soul, and bind them for a sign upon your hand, that they may be as frontlets between your eyes.

And ye shall teach them your children, speaking of them when thou sittest in thine house, and when thou walkest by the way, when thou liest down, and when thou risest up.

And thou shalt write them upon the door posts of thine house, and upon thy gates:

That your days may be multiplied, and the days of your children, in the land which the LORD sware unto your fathers to give them, as the days of heaven upon the earth.

DEUTERONOMY 11:18-21

God gave the Children of Israel an amazing promise of a life of heaven upon the earth. He instructed them to lay up His words in their hearts and in their souls, keeping it constantly before their eyes so that they would constantly remember them and act upon them. If they did, the result would be that their days on earth would be multiplied in the land which God had given them as the days of heaven upon the earth.

This promise of a life of heaven upon the earth was given to the children of Israel when they came out of the land of Egypt and were on their way to possess the land of Canaan.

Though the Land of Canaan was previously occupied by the Canaanites, God promised to give his people the land, furthermore, he revealed to them that if they allowed His word to govern their actions while dwelling in that land, then they would experience life here on earth as though they were already in heaven.

God's plan has always been for man to live on earth as though he was in heaven. This was the reason why Our Lord Jesus Christ taught the twelve Disciples to pray that the will of God should be done on earth as it is being done in heaven.

> Thy kingdom come. Thy will be done in earth, as *it is* in heaven.
>
> MATTHEW 6:10

One of the things that makes heaven a place of bliss is the fact that all those who dwell in heaven do God's will in every aspects of their lives. When we on earth receive and act upon God's word for different aspects of our lives, we will begin to experience heaven in all our affairs.

Marriage is one of God's gifts to man. It was God's idea for Adam to have a wife in the beginning. God designed marriage and planned for it to be a blissful experience; a part of the Eden life he designed for man.

INTRODUCTION

The original Garden where God placed the first couple that ever lived (Adam and Eve) was a paradise; a place of complete joy until man began to listen to Satan's voice and began to do Satan's bidding.

It was not the will of God for Adam and Eve to eat the fruit of the knowledge of good and evil at the time they ate it, this was why he warned them not to eat it. However, they rather chose to listen to the voice of Satan and ate the fruit. They did not realise that they were yielding their God given authority to Satan by obeying him.

Satan gained access to speak into the union of Adam and Eve continuously afterwards and as they continued to yield to him by doing his will, he brought a life of hell upon the earth where Adam and Eve lived.

Through His redemptive work on the cross of Calvary, Our Lord Jesus has again given mankind access to enjoy a life of heaven on the earth through the giving of the Holy Spirit and the revelation of His plan for marriage and relationships.

In this book *'Heaven on Earth in Marriage and Relationships'* you will discover God's plan for Marriage and how He intends for you to conduct yourself in your 'Canaan land' of marriage in order for you to enjoy a life of heaven on earth.

Going into a marriage or relationship is like going into the Land of Canaan. Your experience in the land will be controlled by your obedience to God's voice as well as your partner's. What will make your Canaan land a place of bliss is a decision to do exactly what God commanded Israel to do.

Laying up God's word concerning love and relationship and following the word of God as a road map of how to act in marriage will bring a life of Heaven on Earth into your Marriage.

On the contrary, if you allow this world's system of dealing in relationships dominate you, you will drift away and find yourself stumbling into the zone where Satan makes you live a life of hell on earth in your marriage and relationships.

CHAPTER 1

THE ATMOSPHERE OF HEAVEN IN MARRIAGE & RELATIONSHIPS

Whom have I in heaven *but thee*? and *there is* none upon earth *that* I desire beside thee.

Psalm 73:25

Heaven is a place of Joy and peace. It is a place of blessings, faith and hope. In heaven there is no sorrow.

What defines the atmosphere of heaven is the presence of the Holy Spirit. Think about it, without the Holy Spirit there can be no joy and peace. Without the Holy Spirit there can be no love. The Holy Spirit's presence is what defines the atmosphere of heaven.

Today, God has given us His Holy Spirit so that we can live on earth as though we are in heaven. Yielding to the Holy Spirit holds the key to a blissful marriage. His presence in your life is critical to finding Joy and peace in your relationships.

Many married people have made the mistake of not recognising that the Holy Spirit holds the key to bringing the atmosphere of heaven into their marriage. The Holy Spirit is the special one in heaven. Our Lord Jesus looks as glorious as He does now after His resurrection because the Holy Spirit has glorified Him. Our Lord Jesus is waiting for the church who is described as His bride to be prepared for Him by the same Holy Spirit.

Every man and woman needs to have the presence of the Holy Spirit in manifestation on his or her life every day just like the glory upon Jesus, in order to be the kind of husband or wife that would love in marriage without compromise. It is important to marry someone who is born again, Spirit filled and has a deep relationship with the Holy Spirit, and those who are already married need to seek to be constantly filled and controlled by the Holy Spirit in the actions they take in their marriage.

Anyone who does not have a good relationship with the Holy Spirit will not be able to give true love as he or she ought to do. If the person you are in a relationship with is not currently filled with the Holy Spirit, then you must spend time praying specifically for the Holy Spirit to rest upon them.

If you are filled with the Holy Spirit daily and you constantly seek to please Him, and your partner does the same, the Holy Spirit will grace your lives with His presence and He will bring the atmosphere of heaven into your relationship. The atmosphere of heaven is supposed to pour from the inside of both the husband and the wife in a marriage because that is where the Holy Spirit lives.

Most people place wrong priorities on physical things as keys to success in marriage or relationships, but I dare say to you that what you need to succeed in your marriage or relationship is to seek to become yielded to the Holy Spirit and to allow the Holy Spirit to control all your actions in that relationship.

Without the Holy Spirit no couple can truly be faithful to the marriage vow to love till death do them part and a great deal of unmarried people in relationship end up always fighting till their relationship falls apart. Having the Holy Spirit is one thing but following His voice is another. So many conflicts in relationship are results of people in relationship disobeying the voice of the Holy Spirit.

It is important to note that the Holy Spirit has already spoken all He needs to say to you about marriage in the bible. If you take the bible as the Holy Spirit speaking to you and commit to obeying scriptures as His voice to you, you will surely experience heaven on earth in your marriage.

When we talk about heaven on earth in marriage and relationships, we imply a state of peace, calmness, joy and blessings in your relationships.

So many marriages and relationships can be defined today as battle fields where Satan reigns freely. Once Satan controls the words and actions of any man or woman in any relationship, he brings hell upon the scene.

What makes heaven a place of bliss? It is simply because it is a place where God rules without Satanic interference. To experience heaven in our relationships, we must commit to allowing God's word rule in our actions and dealings with people we are in a relationship with regardless of what the other party does. What makes heaven a place to be desired is that it is a place where Satan's activities, character and effect is absent. Everything about heaven is one hundred percent God.

This reveals to us that if we can operate in our marriages and relationships with one hundred percent of God's rules and principles our relationships will be filled with heavenly bliss. If we can ensure that Satan does not sneak into our conducts or gains control of our thoughts, words and actions; if we can keep Satan away from our relationships then we can be guaranteed of heaven on earth in our marriage.

What makes hell a place of horror is the presence of Satan. Satan's presence brings trauma, as a result many marriages are filled with trauma because the individuals concerned have allowed the devil in through satanic conducts.

When a couple become violent and anger rules over them, when selfishness and pride enter in, and each person strives for supremacy without being willing to yield or submit to the other person; then Satan has gained control and an atmosphere of hell is bound to prevail in such a marriage or relationship.

CHAPTER 2

IMBIBING THE CULTURE AND LIFESTYLE OF HEAVEN

There remaineth therefore a rest to the people of God.

For he that is entered into his rest, he also hath ceased from his own works, as God did from his.

HEBREWS 4:9-10

Spirits define cultures of different geographical locations and environments. The Holy Spirit has created among heaven dwellers a culture of joy, peace, faith, hope, love and fellowship.

This is the culture of heaven and if you will bring heaven into your marriage or relationship, you must choose to be joyful regardless of the circumstance. You must pursue peace and be willing to sacrifice for peace to reign. You must have faith that your spouse or person you are in a relationship with, will change for the better regardless of what you see now and choose to call things that be not as though they were, instead of calling things that are the way they are.

The world's way of living is that unspiritual people are solely controlled by their senses. For example, they say things are not working when they see that things are not working.

You must learn to walk by faith in your relationship; choosing to see your spouse the way God sees them regardless of what attitudes they put on display.

The culture of heaven is that people love by choice. In marriage every couple must know that they have a command from God to love not by feelings only but as an act of obedience to God's command. If you are a wife you must love, be patient, respectful and never allow anger to have the better of you. The same applies to every husband.

If you are unmarried but in a relationship with the hope of getting married, you must learn to practice this principle as otherwise your relationship may not last.

So many people have allowed the devil to drive them into sadness and deep unhappiness in their relationships.

The devil uses offence and unforgiveness to perpetuate deep hurt. He uses malice, a situation where you and the person you are in a relationship with go for days without talking to each other because none of you is willing to submit and be the humble one; and by so doing the devil makes you very unhappy in your relationship.

It is important to know what God expects you to do when you are offended or hurt by the actions of people you love. Firstly, avoid malice and do not let the sun go down on your anger without you trying to resolve your differences.

You must learn to go to the person who offended you and let the person know what they have done that hurt you in the spirit of meekness and forgive them even before they repent. Be patient and persistent, even if the person does not respond positively after your initial efforts at making peace.

The devil will suggest to you to hold on to your hurt and withdraw but if you obey him you will invite hell into the situation.

Hell has its culture. Fear, unforgiveness, keeping a record of wrongs, anger; are all cultural lifestyle of hell dwellers.

Satan is always the one controlling you if you allow fear to control you in your relationship. When fear controls you, you will become a terrorist in your marriage.

If you are afraid that your partner will cheat on you, that fear will make you begin to act like an investigative officer and no one likes to know that they are being watched or investigated.

Fear of any kind in marriage will make you unknowingly terrorise your spouse and he or she would not be able to live freely in your presence because you will become violent out of fear. The result is that your spouse will make more mistakes and be pushed to hide things from you. This is the number one cause of a deep gap between couples. Someone is controlled by fear and anger, and as a result has become a "terrorist" to the other person.

Your spouse may have done somethings in the past that may give you reasons to be aggressive today, but you must decide not to allow such ruin your marriage.

Forgive genuinely and deliberately decide never to remind your spouse of their wrongs if they repeat the same thing again. You need to have faith and hope for the best.

You cannot live with anyone in relationship if you are always negative and literally believe for the worst about the person. Love believes the best about people. Our objective in marriage should be to bring the influence of the Holy Spirit into our behaviour, actions and conduct in our relationships.

HEAVEN AND THE WILL OF GOD

Not every one that saith unto me, Lord, Lord, shall enter into the kingdom of heaven; but he that doeth the will of my Father which is in heaven.

Matthew 7:21

Heaven is a place where the will of God is being done. If you are not committed to doing the will of God, then you must forget about experiencing heaven in your relationships.

This is the reason why many married Christians are not happy in their marriages. The fact that you lift up your hands on Sundays and sing, *'He is Lord, He is Lord'*, to Jesus will not guarantee you bliss in your marriage except you do what

His word commands you to do in that marriage.

Heaven dwellers do not struggle to do God's will. Here on earth, the cause of conflicts in most marriages is that a lot of husbands and wives refuse to recognise God's will regarding their roles in their marriages and are unwilling to yield to obey God's instructions in dealing with their spouse.

The fight for supremacy and the unwillingness to submit one to another in the fear of God in times of difficult conversations results in the marriage being filled with conflicts.

The fact about a life of heaven is that heaven dwellers do the will of God. Most people do mostly their own will and pursue their own plans which really is not theirs but Satan's, so their relationship is filled with hell.

Now someone may say, *'but what if just one partner is doing the will of God and the other partner is not, will there not be an abuse?'*

The fact to note is that your goal in any relationship you are in, should be to please God regardless of how your partner acts. You should focus solely on pleasing God and never fall for the temptation of acting against God's word because your partner is not committed to pleasing God.

You are firstly a Christian before you got into that relationship and you should not begin to act like an unbeliever because you find yourself with someone who is unwilling to please God.

CHAPTER 3

CREATING HEAVEN IN YOUR RELATIONSHIPS

By the word of the LORD were the heavens made; and all the host of them by the breath of his mouth.

PSALM 33:6

The planet called heaven did not come into existent out of nothing. God built or created it with His word and by the breath of his mouth who is the Holy Spirit. A life of heaven on earth is to be created by God's words.

Psalm 33 verse 6 also declares; *'To him that by wisdom made the heavens: for his mercy endureth for ever.'*

This reveals to us that wisdom expressed through right words inspired by the Holy Spirit was the key to the creation of heaven.

How can we create heaven in our marriage or relationships especially when it is currently without form and void and filled with conflicts of different kinds? The answer is simple. By faith, the worlds were framed by the words of God.

In Genesis chapter 1 verse 2, the earth was without form and void and darkness was upon the face of the deep. God did not complain about the situation when he saw it chaotic, instead he spoke. God said let there be light, and light came and displaced the darkness. God released the substance of heaven into the earth.

> Through faith we understand that the worlds were framed by the word of God, so that things which are seen were not made of things which do appear.
>
> HEBREWS 11:3

If you do not see heaven in your marriage you have to begin to speak into it to create what you desire while watching out to stop speaking what you may have been speaking that may have created the chaos.

Heaven was built by God's words and wisdom; your marital bliss can only be built by the same materials of words and wisdom.

An unwise man or woman will use wrong words to create strife and conflicts in his or her relationships. Watch your tongue and ensure that hell fire is not fuelling the words you speak to your spouse or partner.

If you call your spouse ugly names and use derogatory comments, that will bring hell instead of heaven into your marriage.

As simple as this principle is, it is one of the biggest causes of marital failures and conflicts in relationships. Many people have a toxic tongue and they use on just anyone including people they are in a relationship with and by so doing they create hell instead of heaven.

Hell feeds its signals into people's minds through thoughts and once you take Satan's thoughts and speak them to your spouse or partner hell appears on the scene.

PUT THE BLESSING ON YOUR MARRIAGE

And it shall come to pass, when the LORD thy God hath brought thee in unto the land whither thou goest to possess it, **that thou shalt put the blessing** upon mount Gerizim, and the curse upon mount Ebal.

DEUTEORONOMY 11:29

One of the characteristics of heaven is that it is a place filled with blessings. There is no curse or evil occurrence in heaven.

When Israel came out of Egypt and were going into the land of Canaan, God gave them a very important instruction of what they needed to do to the land of Canaan when they arrived there.

He commanded them to put the blessing upon Gerizim and the curse upon mount Ebal. God was revealing that Canaan land was neither blessed nor cursed and the Gerizim aspect of the land that became blessed, got blessed because the blessing was put on it, while the Ebal part that became cursed also became cursed because the curse was put on it.

The land is neither blessed nor cursed, it responds to what you put on it.

When you get married or go into a relationship, it is symbolic of you coming into your Canaan land. Different aspects of your marriage or relationship become blessed or cursed depending on what you put on it.

Put the blessing! Heaven is a place of the blessing. God blesses when He speaks. God's words are impregnated with the blessing. This is why He commanded us to lay up His words in our spirit.

> These shall stand upon mount Gerizim to bless the people, when ye are come over Jordan; Simeon, and Levi, and Judah, and Issachar,
>
> Deuteronomy 27:12

Mount Gerizim is a type of Mount Zion which refers to the life of the born-again believers. Joshua was supposed to bring the people into the land of Canaan and upon arrival they were to put the blessing upon mount Gerizim. Then the tribes of Simeon, Levi, Judah and Issachar were to stand upon the blessed mountain and proclaim the blessing over the people.

Jesus is to us what Joshua was to Israel and He has not only brought us into the spiritual land of Canaan, He has also put the blessing upon us according to the words of Acts 3:26.

Unto you first God, having raised up his Son Jesus, sent him to bless you, in turning away every one of you from his iniquities.

Acts 3:26

When they put the blessing upon Mount Gerizim the mountain became blessed and from thence, they were to stand upon that blessed mountain and communicate the blessing once the blessing is placed on it to the whole nation. Today, you are blessed and have been made a communicator of the blessing. You have to walk in this consciousness every time you speak to your spouse or partner.

God commanded the people to stand on the blessed mountain and bless the people. We are as Gerizim is today. Jesus has put the blessing upon us, now we have the responsibility of standing on the blessing by faith and putting those same blessings on people around us and upon every work of our hands.

God has given us His words with which to use to put the blessing. We put the blessing by correcting our spouses in love when they make mistakes instead of shouting at them with a negative angry spirit.

Your words are your blessing agent. When you speak to your spouse or partner you should endeavour to communicate the blessing to them in every situation. Why is it important to put the blessing? Putting the blessing is you bringing heaven into your marriage or relationship.

There is already a curse out there in the world. Many couples are living in strife and conflicts and they want a way out of it. You can choose to build a different system in your home. When you speak loving words and constantly declare the blessing over your spouse to their hearing, change comes into marriage.

We have the responsibility to put the blessing upon our marriages, our jobs, our homes, our children.

When Adam was first created, he was neither blessed nor cursed until God put the blessing on him.

> So God created man in his own image, in the image of God created he him; male and female created he them.
>
> And God blessed them, and God said unto them, Be fruitful, and multiply, and replenish the earth, and subdue it: and have dominion over the fish of the sea, and over the fowl of the air, and over every living thing that moveth upon the earth.
>
> Genesis 1:27-28

Similarly, a marriage is neither blessed nor cursed at inception. What a marriage becomes is dependent on whether the participants in that marriage put either the blessing or the curse on their marriage.

God blessed Adam and Eve by speaking words over them. In the same way we put the blessing upon things with our words.

When God said concerning you that *"In you shall all nations be blessed."* He implied that in you shall your family be blessed. Do not stand and watch your family go in a direction you do not desire. Put the blessing on them. Do not stand and watch your car behave in the way you do not desire for it to behave. Put the blessing on it.

Do not stand and watch your marriage or relationship go down the conflict route. Put the blessing upon it.

In you shall all nations be blessed. Means all nations are waiting for you to bless them. Your company is waiting for you to put the blessing upon it. Stop complaining about your job and start putting the blessing upon it.

Put the blessing upon your bank accounts by speaking to it.

It is important to state that just as we are required to put the blessing, it is possible that you may actually be putting a curse upon yourself rather than the blessing if you engage in speaking outside of line with what God's word says.

Watch the words that you speak. Make sure that you expect what you say to come to pass. Every idle word that you speak works just as much as the words you speak deliberately. Make sure you are putting the blessing on your life and not a curse.

CHAPTER 4

THE LAW OF RESPECT IN RELATIONSHIPS

And as the ark of the LORD came into the city of David, Michal Saul's daughter looked through a window, and saw king David leaping and dancing before the LORD; and she despised him in her heart.

Then David returned to bless his household. And Michal the daughter of Saul came out to meet David, and said, How glorious was the king of Israel to day, who uncovered himself to day in the eyes of the handmaids of his servants, as one of the vain fellows shamelessly uncovereth himself!

And David said unto Michal, *It was* before the LORD, which chose me before thy father, and before all his house, to appoint me ruler over the people of the LORD, over Israel: therefore will I play before the LORD.

And I will yet be more vile than thus, and will be base in mine own sight: and of the maidservants which thou hast spoken of, of them shall I be had in honour. Therefore Michal the daughter of Saul had no child unto the day of her death. 2 SAMUEL 6:16, 20 – 23

HEAVEN ON EARTH IN MARRIAGE

The law of respect in relationships can simply be defined as your ability to recognise the value or worth of a person and treating such a person based on your evaluation of the person's esteemed worth regardless of the circumstances.

Michal the daughter of Saul was David's wife. She momentarily lost sight of the fact that David was the Anointed King of Israel when she exhibited total dishonour towards him.

The scripture records that she sharply reprimanded David because David danced publicly before the ark of the covenant of God. In her opinion, dancing in such a way as David did publicly did not befit him as a king and she despised David in her heart as a result. The bible in Easy English translation of that verse records that she called David *'a silly fool'*, and that really offended David.

As a result of this art of disrespect by Michal, the scripture records that she had no more children till the day that she died. I believe David did not have any sexual relationships with her anymore because of her act of disrespect to him.

Michal fell into the trap that a lot of people in relationships fall into frequently that literarily destroys their relationships. She lost sight of the fact that David was not just her husband but the Anointed King of Israel. No one who is conscious of the fact that David was the anointed King of Israel would dare publicly criticize or speak against the King the way Michal did.

Most relationships and marriages usually start out because a man esteems a lady highly and vice versa, however most

THE LAW OF RESPECT IN RELATIONSHIPS

people allow familiarity to begin to breed contempt in them when they become used to their partners.

Like Michal did, many couples call their spouses names like *'silly fool'*, while some even go further to use more abusive words to address their spouses when they are displeased with them.

The fact that you are displeased with your spouse's actions does not authorise you to act or speak disrespectfully to them.

Words are vehicles for showing respect or disrespect depending on the kind of words you speak. Addressing your spouse with derogatory names is one the most ignoble act any married man or woman can engage in.

Being respectful is a virtue that must be imbibed if you want to enjoy a life of heaven on earth in your marriage or relationships. The Law of respect is a powerful force that affects most relationships without most people recognising that their acts of disrespect is costing them a lot. What you disrespect will move away from you.

RESPECT OPENS DOORS OF ACCESS

Respect opens up doors of access while disrespect shuts doors to many unknowingly. When a woman treats her husband with respect, she gains access to everything he has without limitations. Similarly, when a man treats his wife with respect, she becomes driven to constantly pour herself into him.

Michal could not have children because she disrespected the man who was supposed to make her bear children.

Similarly, many wives have shut down their emotions towards their husbands and vice versa because most couples are guilty of walking disrespectfully towards each other. Sex dies where disrespect exists. Most couples are suffering sexually, primarily because they have conducted themselves disrespectfully towards one another.

Pride is usually at the root of all forms of disrespect. You can see that pride is at work because even when disrespectful people are corrected, they do not accept their faults, they never apologize for their errors but rather seek to justify their acts of disrespect.

Michal never apologized to David for calling him a silly fool and as a result her marital relationship with David literarily ended. Are you wondering why your sexual life has dried up?

When you and your partner go for several days without sex or when your sexual life is no more appealing, you need to check up on how respectfully you have been treating each other.

Are you a disrespectful person? Your acts of disrespect are hurting you in unimaginable ways.

A great deal of people suffer primarily because they are disrespectful to the authority figures in their lives. What you respect you treat with regard and extra courtesy.

Honour all *men*. Love the brotherhood. Fear God. Honour the king.

1Peter 2:17

THE LAW OF RESPECT IN RELATIONSHIPS

The scripture commands us to honour all men as a primary way of life. Whether the person in question is your spouse, your children or a servant who works for you; everyone deserves the right to be honoured and respected.

Have you noticed that when an honourable man or person comes to your house you treat the person with some extra courtesy and are even willing to sacrifice for such a person to be comfortable?

The fuel that keeps the fire of sacrifice in marriage burning is constantly walking in respect and honour towards your partner. You cannot have real marriage if both of you do not sacrifice for each other. You will be willing to sacrifice for any person you honour to be comfortable because you honour them.

However, when you become unduly familiar with your spouse, you will find that you will literally throw away that extra courtesy and begin to be disrespectful in your words and actions. You will no longer be willing to sacrifice when you have no respect for your partner neither will you be tolerant anymore.

To walk in respect means to honour and esteem people in your life highly. Make it a principle of your life to always treat all men beginning with people who are close to you with some extra courtesy!

When you are respectful, you tend to be more tolerant. You do not shout at any person who you hold in high esteem; even when the person misbehaves, you tend to tolerate the person's errors because of your respect for the person.

Being respectful makes you tolerant!

Respect is measured by how you treat people, your manner of communication and attitude towards them.

Your manner of communication should never reflect rudeness or sarcasm. Responding with sarcastic answers when you are asked questions or a body language that clearly states *'I have no regard for you or your presence'* will quickly destroy your relationships.

A lot of married couples struggle to find domestic helpers to work for them in their homes because they treat their helpers with complete dishonour. You must learn to honour all men including your domestic workers.

RESPECT MAKES YOU CONTROL YOUR ANGER

Everyone gets angry at one point in time or the other. Anyone you are in a relationship with will make you angry. However, many people completely become different at those times of provocation and begin to act in regrettable ways primarily by losing sight of the principle of respect.

> And Elisha said, As the LORD of hosts liveth, before whom I stand, surely, were it not that I regard the presence of Jehoshaphat the king of Judah, I would not look toward thee, nor see thee.
>
> 2KINGS 3:14

Elisha was provoked to anger by the actions of the King of Israel. When the Kings of Israel, Judah and Moab came to meet him for help, Elisha did not want to look towards the king of Israel or even see his face. However, because he had respect for the King of Judah he managed his anger towards the king of Israel and did what they asked for.

This is how respect should affect your reactions. Do not go overboard in your reactions in anger when you are dealing with someone who means a lot to you; learn to respond to them because you have regard for them.

If perhaps you are currently facing challenges in your relationship, it is important to examine your manner of communication and attitude and decide to quit being abusive and become more cautious when you speak. Speak with regard and awareness that you are talking to your spouse or someone you love. When you do you will immediately see a change coming into your relationship.

God made you to be an honourable person and not a dishonourable person so refuse to let the devil make you practice walking in dishonour.

What you respect you give attention to! Most men are victims of ignoring their wives needs and fail to give the right attention.

One attitude that demonstrates that you respect someone is when you give face to face attention to the person when the person is speaking to you.

You hear things like, *'I am talking to you'*, being shouted by people in relationship because the other person is simply not giving the attention that proves respect to the person speaking. Where your treasure is, there your heart will be. If you respect your partner, you will give him or her attention.

RESPECT BREEDS RESPECT

Have you noticed how quickly people readily insult you back when you insult them? The rule is that respect breeds respect while disrespect breeds disrespect through the law of seeds.

The bible states that whatsoever a man sows the same shall he reap.

Never forget this; what you disrespect generally moves away from you. That is the reason why many girls and guys cannot keep a relationship for long, and also the reason why many marriages are falling apart today; because what you disrespect will move away from you.

Watch your tongue! Be careful of how you use it. The tongue is the means for all forms of verbal expressions. You express love through words. You also express honour or dishonour with words. There are some words you should never use against anyone you love.

Watch your tone of voice when communicating. Your tone of voice carries a message with it.

When you shout at your spouse or anyone, the person doesn't just hear what you said but also your tone of voice tells the person that you do not honour such a person and that you have no respect for them.

It is important to train yourself to speak respectfully to people generally. People will like you if you are a very respectful person.

RESPECT AND ANGER MANAGEMENT

To walk in respect towards people in your life you will have to learn to manage your anger.

When you shout at people one key reason is because you are angry. You could have become angry because your expectations were not met or because you simply have an anger problem; however, if unchecked that anger will drive you into disrespect.

One cure for anger is found in the following scripture;

Be not hasty in thy spirit to be angry: for anger resteth in the bosom of fools.

ECCLESIASTES 7:9

Anger rests in the bosom of fools! Every time you are about to become angry, quickly remind yourself that you are not a fool and shouldn't become one because anger rests in the bosom of fools.

CHAPTER 5

THE LAW OF RECOGNITION IN RELATIONSHIPS

And Adam said, this is now bone of my bones, and flesh of my flesh: she shall be called Woman, because she was taken out of Man.

GENESIS 2:23

The law of recognition was one of the first principles employed by Adam as he established a relationship with Eve; it is also the key to success in marriage and relationship today.

Adam recognised the physical looks of Eve. He called her bone of his bones and flesh of his flesh. The scripture then declared, *'therefore shall a man leave his father and his mother and shall cleave unto his wife.'*

This action of leaving and cleaving was triggered by the law of recognition. When a man recognises his wife's values, beauty and essence, it becomes very easy for him to cleave to her.

The same is true in every aspect of human life. Most people hang around people of value, essence and worth. If you do not see the value or worth of a person you would hardly want to invest your time into a relationship with such a person.

For single people who are still trying to decide on going into a relationship, it is important to establish a right basis for attraction. Sexual appeal is not enough for you to decide to spend the rest of your life with someone.

Starting from the God factor, you and whoever you want to be in a relationship with, must connect spiritually. If you are on different spiritual planes, there is a high probability that even though you are sexually attracted to each other you will have problems because of the spiritual difference between both of you. Be attracted for good reasons.

For Adam we see that part of the reason why Eve was attracted to him was because she was just from God. God formed her and brought her to him.

> And the rib, which the LORD God had taken from man, made he a woman, and brought her unto the man.
>
> GENESIS 2:22

Imagine meeting someone who has just been worked on by

THE LAW OF RECOGNITION IN RELATIONSHIPS

God and was coming from God's presence for the first time. Everything about such a person will be attractive to you.

If you are already in relationship, you should work on developing a good relationship with God and allow God to work in you in order to stay attractive.

We also note that as a result of Adam's recognition of Eve's sexual appeal, the scripture recorded that they were both naked and were not ashamed.

Verbally recognising your spouse's physical look and sexual appeal on an on-going basis is the secret to a vibrant sexual life.

If you are a married man, you will have noticed that your wife always asks you about how she looks after she dresses up, this is so because recognising and complimenting her looks is one of the biggest things that releases and unlocks her sexuality.

God designed the woman to be responsive in nature. Eve became all that Adam spoke about her, bone of his bones and flesh of his flesh.

> And they were both naked, the man and his wife, and were not ashamed.
>
> GENESIS 2:25

The Hebrew word translated *'ashamed'* in Genesis 2:25 is the word *'boosh'* and one of its meanings is to *'become dry'*.

Adam and Eve were naked, and their sexual relationship

did not become dry because Adam used the law of recognition to lubricate it.

To constantly lubricate your relationship, it is important for you to constantly recognise the physical looks of your spouse.

Words play a critical role in our everyday lives. Right words create the right atmosphere in any place. People draw closer to you if you speak right words whereas wrong words could create a void and make even people who love you drift away from you.

Do not wait for your spouse to ask for compliments before you give it. Adam was forward with complimenting Eve. Eve did not request for compliments before he gave it. Similarly, we must not wait to be asked before we pass compliments. Ladies need to recognise that the men in their lives also need to be made to feel that they are the right men for them.

Complimenting a man helps him to take his place as a man.

RECOGNITION OF YOUR SPOUSES CONCEPT OF LOVE

Every woman has a unique love need. Most men fall into the trap of treating their wives like their mothers or their junior sisters.

If you are a married man, it is important to recognise the fact that your wife is different from every other woman you may have had in your life. Avoid falling into the subtle trap

THE LAW OF RECOGNITION IN RELATIONSHIPS

of attempting to treat her like the other women you have known.

Find out what makes your wife happy and when she tells you, give attention to it.

Similarly, if you are a married woman, it is also important for you to recognise your husband's concept of love. To a lot of men talking to them with respect and being submissive to them is the proof that you love them.

Everyone has expectations when it comes to their concept of love. It is important for you and your spouse to spend time educating each other on your expectations.

Never assume that the other person knows how to love you.

Some women say things like, *'if he doesn't know how to make a woman happy, he should go and ask his friends'*. In most cases the man in question may be trying his best to please his wife but because the woman has failed to educate him on exactly what her concept of love is, the man ends up being frustrated. The same also applies to the men. Many ladies are feeling frustrated because the husbands do not appreciate their efforts at loving them.

If is important to educate each other on what you expect from your partner. Never assume that your spouse should know how to treat you.

I always love to say that every husband and wife in a marriage, come into that marital relationship as apprentices. Your spouse has never been married to you before, he or she therefore needs your help to succeed in understanding your love needs and meeting them.

SENSITIVITY TO THE EMOTIONAL NEEDS OF YOUR SPOUSE

Be sensitive to each other's emotional needs. There are times when different emotional winds blow and cause a man or a woman to be emotionally weak. It is good practice not to mock or despise the person who may be going through that emotional swing but to show care and concern even if you believe your spouse may be overreacting.

A soft answer always turns away anger. It also pacifies a wounded or hurting person. Do not focus on whether a person is justified to feel the way he or she feels emotionally but rather focus on bringing healing to such a person at such a time through kind words.

RECOGNITION OF YOUR SPOUSES PERSPECTIVE OF VIEW

Your spouse or whoever you are in relationship with, reserves the right to have a voice and an opinion different from yours. This is one core reason why you need one another. However, the devil can make this become the basis for your constant fighting if you fail to recognise the value of your partner's perspective of view.

What defines a person's perspective of view is their upbringing. Do not criticize or wonder about why your spouse or partner should view things differently from the way you do.

He or she was wired differently and your difference in views is the reason why you need each other. Respect the difference in opinion and learn to allow the principle of

THE LAW OF RECOGNITION IN RELATIONSHIPS

submitting yourselves one to another to reign in your engagements.

Many couples fight because of their difference in viewing things instead of respecting and celebrating each other more for the different ways they analyse things. Your difference is your asset, prize it.

RECOGNITION OF YOUR SPOUSES OPINION IN DECISION MAKING

Don't decide without your spouse's knowledge. Unilateral decisions could hurt your relationship. Make it a practice to always consult with your partner before making financial decisions.

A common mistake that occurs is that many couples operate separately when it comes to their finances. The man has his money and the woman has her money and they make financial decisions because they believe it is their money.

Selfishness and greed are mostly at the root of the situations where couples operate separate financial purses. The right order is that you and your spouse are supposed to be one financially. The true proof of maturity is the ability to do things together without resorting to a fight.

Someone may say, *'but she will not allow me to do what I want to do for my family members if I am open to her financially.'* You are being unwise if you do not involve your wife or husband in your financial decisions.

You are supposed to be one flesh according to the word of God and you should be one in every way.

The problem with most people is that they are unwilling to defend their decisions. If you believe that your decision is right, then you should not be afraid for it to be scrutinized by your partner.

We all need speed breaks in our lives to keep us from going into excesses. Allow your spouse to be the speed break in your areas of excesses.

RECOGNITION OF THE BENEFIT OF CRITICISM

Criticisms opens your minds to what you may not have paid attention to if you allow it. Be open to criticisms and do not take it with a bad attitude.

People who are averse to being criticised are suffering from inferiority complex. Your spouse should be able to criticise you without you taking offence at his or her criticism. If you want to improve in life you must learn to receive criticisms with a good attitude.

Some people see those who criticize their ideas or opinions as though they do not like them while others take criticisms as attacks on their personality. You should always learn to separate your personality from your ideas. When people criticize your ideas do not take it is an attack on your personality.

The key to improving in life is recognising where people are better than you and learning from them. You should always look out for the value that your partner is trying to add to you rather than allowing the devil to use his or her effort at helping you improve as a tool for provocation.

THE LAW OF RECOGNITION IN RELATIONSHIPS

RECOGNITION OF THE BENEFIT OF OPENNESS

Openness and transparency in all your dealings is a key lubricant to your marriage. Avoid hiding things from your spouse. When you hide things, you create room for suspicion and conflicts to occur when the truth is revealed, and always remember that anything you hide will always come into the limelight sooner or later.

Always remember this scripture;

> For there is nothing hid, which shall not be manifested; neither was any thing kept secret, but that it should come abroad.
>
> MARK 4:22

When you hide things from your spouse, you open yourself to the spirit of fear in your marriage. The fear of being caught will take hold of you and make you begin to act deceptively. Fear draws the devil upon the scene just as faith pulls God into the situation.

Be open and transparent. Tell the truth all the time regardless of whether you will be crucified for it. It is better to be crucified for being truthful than to become a lying hypocrite.

As a person, it is important to learn to create an atmosphere that will encourage our partners to be open and transparent with us. One way is to manage your reaction when your partner opens up to you. Avoid being judgemental when your spouse reveals a weakness to you. If a decision is made and you are informed at a later stage, do not start a fight about why you were not informed before the decision because it will make the concerned person afraid to inform you the next time such occurs. Instead, if necessary correct in love and always encourage transparency.

On the flip side, always know that being judged or crucified by your spouse is not a reason to become secretive. Take the bashing but remain open and transparent.

RECOGNITION OF THE POWER OF WORDS

Recognition of the power of words and using them appropriately is an important key to enjoying a life of heaven on earth in your relationship.

Words are spirit! Words, when used rightly give life in a relationship the exact same way that the physical body of a man receives life from the human spirit of the man.

Words are vehicles! Words are spiritual and emotional transport vehicles. Words can injure or heal. What you say brings joy or sorrow to your hearers depending on how you say it. Always ask yourself what your motive is every time you use specific words.

Words can pacify or provoke depending on how you use them. Words can instruct or harden the heart of your spouse towards you.

Words are like water, once spilled you cannot recoup or recall them. It is therefore important to be slow to speak and avoid using words that will hurt which you may never be able to recall back. If you use hurting words on your spouse during times of conflicts, when you try to make peace those words will continue to ring a bell in their minds.

CHAPTER 6

PRESERVING FRIENDSHIP & MAGNETISM

And when he had been there for some time, Abimelech, king of the Philistines, looking through a window, saw Isaac playing with Rebekah his wife. Bible in Basic English Translation

GENESIS 26:8

The relationship between Isaac and Rebekah was a remarkable one. They had such a unique connection and the bible records that the Philistines saw Isaac playing with Rebekah his wife.

They certainly had a friendship relationship in their marriage. One of the keys to preserving friendship in your relationships is finding something both of you can do together. You have to be deliberate about this because if you do not, you may find yourselves drifting apart.

The relationship started with friendship and must be preserved by working hard to ensure you do not drift apart.

Find something to do together. Most men can have long on-going conversations with their friends because they share somethings in common. For example, men who love watching football never get tired of analysing a football match when they are with their friends.

The same rule applies in relationship. It is important to make the effort to love and take interest in what your spouse is interested in.

Find something both of you can do together, talk about together, watch the news together.

You can build friendship more easily if both of you have similar passions and goals. Friendship dies when you cannot find something to do together. Sex becomes like a duty because you are not friends.

Don't change your roles after marriage, remain and maintain the friendship as a basis of relating. Deliberately go out together the way you used to do when you were still courting before marriage. You need to consciously strive to continue doing the things you used to do together before marriage that created a bond between both of you.

Who is a friend? A friend is a confidant. Someone you literally tell everything that happens in your life to. To sustain friendship in your relationship you must constantly communicate and keep your partner in confidence on things happening in your life.

PRESERVING FRIENDSHIP & MAGNETISM

A friend is someone who would give you unsolicited assistance and supports most of your actions. In relationship we must strive to constantly assist our partners where we can before they ask and when they ask we should provide assistance with joy.

A friend is someone you always want to hear from and you offer your attention to your friend most times with a lot of courtesy. If you offer your ears to listen to your partner, you will strengthen your friendship.

A Synonym of the word friend is the word advocate. It implies that your friend will always back your actions and defend you in the face of attacks. To preserve friendship in your relationship, learn to back your spouse's actions and defend them when you find yourself needing to do so. Never take sides with anyone against your wife or husband.

Defend your partner when he or she is under attack from extended family members or from any other source. Always defend your partner first, whether he or she is right or wrong. You can always bring correction to him or her later in private, but in public you must defend first.

If your partner is in the wrong, encourage him or her to go and apologise and right their wrongs. Good friends always encourage each other to do what is right.

MAGNETISM IN MARRIAGE & RELATIONSHIPS

Magnetism is the irresistible pull in a person's life. Concerning marriage every couple gets married based on a certain magnetic factor.

Something in the husband captivated the wife and vice versa that it led to marriage.

In the course of marriage, a great deal of people lose their magnetism unknowingly which causes most couples to drift apart. To sustain your magnetism in your marriage or relationship, the first thing to do is to identify what your magnetic factors are.

The best way to identify your magnetic factor is for the person who was attracted to you to tell you what attracted them to you in the first place. Ask your spouse to tell you the things that appealed to him or her in the beginning. Ask your spouse to critically tell you the truth if you are still as magnetic as in the beginning and ask your spouse what he or she would love you to do to sustain that charm.

On your part, try to identify what you were used to doing that you have stopped doing and make a quality decision to adjust with the objective of reinventing your magnetism. Become a persuasive, charismatic and captivating love magnet. Send love notes, do things that would make your partner want to be around you.

To recreate a magnetic love field around you, you need to put in some effort and the first and most important way to achieve this is to start by using the right words to create what you desire to see.

Love is expressed through words. God is love but we only know His love through His charming, gracious and soul lifting words spoken to us.

PRESERVING FRIENDSHIP & MAGNETISM

If you want to create a magnetic love field around you, you must do something about the words you speak.

Your words must be charming, full of grace and always soul lifting.

No man or woman would want to spend time around someone who tells them how ugly they are all the time. One reason why a lot of couples have drifted apart is because they have used words wrongly against one another.

HOW TO KNOW IF YOUR MARRIAGE HAS LOST ITS MAGNETISM

Does your spouse always want to be around you? If your spouse is uncomfortable being around you, then your attractiveness has diminished.

Do you always want your spouse to be around you? If your spouse doesn't want you to always be around them it could imply that your attractiveness has diminished.

Does your spouse always want to be away from you? Do you always wish your spouse leaves the house?

Does your spouse still look physically handsome or beautiful to you? Many married couples are guilty of not continuing putting in the effort they used to put into ensuring that they look beautiful and handsome and smell nice. It is important to work on your appearance and smell.

The sense of smell is one of the greatest things that can make your sex life magnetic.

CHAPTER 7

GRACE BASED LOVE

For this is as the waters of Noah unto me: for as I have sworn that the waters of Noah should no more go over the earth; so have I sworn that I would not be wroth with thee, nor rebuke thee.

ISAIAH 54:9

In the New Testament God made a different Covenant with us called the covenant of grace.

In this New Covenant, God said in Isaiah 54:9 that He will not be angry with you or rebuke you. He also said in Hebrews 8:12 That He will not remember your sins or keep a record of them.

This is the kind of Love we enjoy from God.

Under the covenant of the law, anger was the order of the day. The disobedience and failures of Israel to fulfil the requirements of the law generated anger.

God decided to seize to be angry with us for our failures because of Jesus' action on the cross for us.

For those of you who think that God is angry with you because of your sins, it is important to state that, that is a lie from the devil himself designed to kill your confidence in approaching God. God is not angry with you.

You need to repent from what you may have done so that you can regain your confidence in approaching Him.

Jesus took all God's anger towards our sins when He was wounded for our transgressions on the cross.

Now we can believe in God's love and relate with other people the same way.

Anger is one reason why many relationships are going through crisis today. The reason for anger is because you are basing your love in that relationship on whether the person fulfils all your expectations like the Law of Moses did.

God wants you to act like Him by choosing not to be angry anymore and love by giving grace; unmerited favours to people in your life who do not deserve it.

Imagine if you choose that in your relationships you will never be angry no matter what people do to you? Also, that you will not keep a record of their sins? think about what your relationships will be like?

GRACE BASED LOVE

God has given you the capacity to live like this by putting His love inside your Spirit.

> And hope does not put to shame; because our hearts are full of the love of God through the Holy Spirit which is given to us.
>
> Romans 5:5

God wants you to live and conduct your life with love that is so gracious. Someone may say, *'but I will be abused if I love like you say.'* Yes, it is possible that you may be abused if you chose to walk by grace just like many of us abuse God's grace, but that is why this love inspired grace is so forgiving.

It forgives those who abuse it even before they repent. Think about how many times you hurt God and yet He remains faithful to you. This is exactly how we ought to relate with people we love. God forgives us primarily because He loves us. God's love for us is the reason behind His grace being demonstrated towards us.

THE PHILOSOPHY OF LOVE

> For I will be merciful to their unrighteousness, and their sins and their iniquities will I remember no more.
>
> HEBREWS 8:12

God is love and grace is His philosophy. Grace in the light of God's promise to be merciful to our unrighteousness and not to remember our sins anymore means unmerited favours.

The philosophy of grace in marriage or relationships simply means treating your spouse or partner with unmerited favours. Giving to your partner what he or she does not deserve in a good way.

There are many things anyone you are in a relationship with will do that may cause you to feel like treating them badly. However, if you imbibe the philosophy of grace you will always treat them well even though they do not deserve it.

Grace is God's chosen way to dealing with us today. It is His mental disposition towards us. In order for us to enjoy a life of heaven upon the earth in our relationships, we need to adopt this philosophy of heaven into our daily lives.

There was a time when God required people to earn their rewards. Under the Law, men got blessed if their deeds were right while they faced the wrath of the law when their deeds were wrong. At that time, the governing rule was an eye for an eye, a tooth for a tooth. You basically receive what you deserve whether good or bad.

When Jesus came He revealed a new philosophy and a new spiritual disposition of God towards man. For example, the Law required the woman caught in adultery to be stoned to death, but grace rather discharged her; declaring her free from condemnation even though she did not deserve it. Grace forgave and cancelled her charges without her asking for forgiveness.

The philosophy of grace under the New Covenant is revealed in this one simple verse of Scripture; *'I will be merciful to their unrighteousness and their sins and their iniquities will I remember no more.'*

Let us understand these two philosophies clearly. Under the law anger was the result of disobedience or non-compliance with the written codes of the law and the outcome of anger were quite devastating. Anger is one of the root causes of crisis in most relationships today. The ladies get angry because of the actions of the men in their lives, the wives do the same to their husbands and vice versa. Anger is an indication that you are operating under the philosophy of the law towards your spouse or partner.

Law minded people in relationship only give others what they deserve, and they have expectations which must be met. If you fail to meet those expectations, such people, like the law would change their countenance towards you.

On the contrary people operating with the philosophy of grace act quite differently. Grace minded people will love you irrespective of what you do. Grace minded people may not be pleased with your actions, but they do not withdraw their kindness because of what you do. They are like their father the God of all grace who causes the sun to shine both on the wicked and the righteous.

Grace minded people believe that you will change no matter how long it takes. Grace minded people are willing to be patient with you, being kind to you when you do not deserve it while they believe for you to change.

Grace minded people do not show you kindness so that you can change, rather grace shows you kindness because its philosophy is to be kind whether you change or not. God changed His way of dealing with us from law to grace. He changed because of Jesus. Jesus took our punishment, so we can receive unmerited favours. As a result of God changing, He has also changed us. We are now no more disposed to breaking His laws and even when we do break those laws, He is still merciful to our transgressions and we repent easily because of His mercy.

If you are married or in a relationship, I encourage you to change. Stop trying to change your partner, God stopped trying to get natural Israel to keep the laws because they just couldn't keep those laws. God changed His philosophy and by doing so we got saved and now what the law could not do because it was weak through the flesh, God Has accomplished by deciding to treat us with grace.

You can change your partner faster if you choose to start treating him or her with grace rather than what he or she deserves. Forgive, correct the faults of your partner in love, and focus on how you can be a blessing to him or her.

I pray that the Holy Spirit will reveal the principle of grace mindedness in your relationship to you in Jesus name.

THE CHARACTER OF GRACE IN RELATIONSHIP

For the grace of God that bringeth salvation hath appeared to all men,

Teaching us that, denying ungodliness and worldly lusts, we should live soberly, righteously, and godly, in this present world;

TITUS 2:11-12

Grace is a teacher! Every time grace appears, it's first line of action is to teach. It patiently teaches its spouse and brings his or her spouse into knowledge of himself/herself.

No two people can truly know themselves in marriage as they ought until they first recognise the need to be transparent with each other.

It is necessary to understand that the teaching nature of Grace does not hide nor withhold anything from the other party.

If you have a weakness in your life, do not be afraid to expose your areas of weaknesses to your spouse and talk about it to him or her. Once you do, you help the person to know you better and know how to help you.

The character of grace is never to be judgemental!

As your partner unveils different aspects of his or her life that might be new to you, be careful not to become judgemental. Learn to respect your spouse's honesty and never use information given to you freely against them.

CHAPTER 8

BRINGING THE GOD KIND OF LOVE INTO YOUR RELATIONSHIPS

Beloved, let us love one another: for love is of God; and every one that loveth is born of God, and knoweth God.

He that loveth not knoweth not God; for God is love.

In this was manifested the love of God toward us, because that God sent his only begotten Son into the world, that we might live through him.

1JOHN 4:7-9

God is love, He is the originator of affection and care. Satan has created for the world a different type of love, different from what God who is love stands for.

Most people base their relationships or marriage on selfishness. Selfishness is a perversion of true love.

Selfishness primarily lives for its own good and seeks its own advantage. Most relationships today are going through crisis because the parties in those relationships are governed by selfishness.

What is selfishness and how does it affect relationships today? Selfishness in relationship simply means going into a relationship FISHING FOR YOURSELF!

Selfish people in relationship always find themselves angry in their relationships when their desires or expectations are not met. Selfishness in relationship makes you aggressive and violent and is the root of relationship crisis.

Being selfish in relationship is being in it for what you can get rather than what you can give; and most times it puts undue pressure on the other party because he or she never seems to be able to satisfy you.

Selfish people are always about themselves and it reflects in their words and actions. It's always about what you didn't do for them and what you did to them that hurt them.

Selfish people never think about what they did to you that was hurting and what they failed to do that they ought to have done.

The difference between this type of love and the God kind of love is that the God kind of love goes into relationship primarily to give to you.

BRINGING THE GOD KIND OF LOVE INTO YOUR RELATIONSHIPS

Are you in a relationship? Would you be able to say that you are selfless or selfish in that relationship? Examine yourself today and if you find that you are selfish, decide to change.

Think daily about what you can give or do to make that person you are in a relationship with happy. Be more consumed with giving rather than getting.

> Herein is love, not that we loved God, but that he loved us, and sent his Son to be the propitiation for our sins.
>
> 1JOHN 4:10

God loved us and gave His son for us, so we can have a different life. He loved us when we were sinful and did acts that were detestable. He loved us when we were unqualified for his love.

He gave us love when we did not ask for it. He loved us while we were still sinners. This is true love. God wants us to love this way just as He loved us.

I encourage you to bring the God kind of love into your relationships. Love in that relationship not because the object of your love deserves it, but because you have the driving force of grace propelling you to do so.

CHAPTER 9

CONFLICT RESOLUTION

Only by pride cometh contention: but with the well advised is wisdom.

PROVERBS 13:10

One of the common threats to several marriages today is strife or contentions. Most men and women find themselves where they are constantly quarrelling with their spouses in their homes.

This strife has created a void between people in relationship. Most couples have grown apart as a result of continuous conflicts.

While each person feels justified in putting up a fight for supremacy in that relationship it is important to bring to your attention the following facts about conflicts in relationship.

CONFLICTS DRAIN YOUR ENERGY

People who engage in quarrels and fights find themselves drained spiritually and exhausted both mentally and physically. The measure of negative effect that conflict in your relationship brings on your spiritual life as well as on you mentally and physically is certainly not worth it.

CONFLICTS AFFECT YOUR PRAYER LIFE

When you fight or quarrel in your relationship your prayer life immediately becomes affected because you would not be able to pray anymore. When you view this negative effect in the light of the scripture, you will discover that in every conflict, there is a hidden hand of Satan.

Satan uses the difference between two of you to generate a fight with an ultimate objective of destroying your prayer life and your relationship with God.

Once you lose your peace and you are unable to connect with God in prayer and fellowship, everything else in your life will begin to fall apart.

SATAN IS BEHIND EVERY CONFLICT

In order for you to deal with that conflict in your relationship you must first recognize that Satan is actually behind it and his objective is to steal your happiness.

CONFLICT RESOLUTION

Regardless of what your partner or spouse may have done or may be doing that you think may be causing the conflict, it is simply Satan behind the scenes and making you see your partner as the cause instead of seeing the devil as the root cause of the problem.

When you therefore engage and entertain the conflict, you are unknowingly working with Satan to destroy what God has blessed you with.

CONFLICTS CREATES ABUSE OF TIME

The time you spend in contending with one another in that relationship is not worth it. You will notice that once there is a conflict between you and your partner, it completely affects your ability to function.

While at work, it destabilizes you and you begin to find it difficult to function well because you engage in a lot of mental activity as you think about what is happening.

Time is being abused and that does not profit you. Time is irreplaceable, you cannot afford to waste crucial aspects of your life on fights that will add no value to your life.

HOW TO ADDRESS THE CONFLICT

To address the conflict that may be in your relationship we need to first identify the root cause.

While everyone in relationship has very clear and genuine reasons that they can put forward as to why their relationship is going through much storms, the book of proverbs reveals a core reason for conflicts in relationships.

Only by pride cometh contention, proverbs 13 verse10 declares.

This is an absolute statement; it reveals that though you may have your reason why you are at war in your relationship those reasons exist because of pride.

Pride is the primary and only reason for conflicts in relationships. Contention is a synonym for the word conflict, and it reveals a rivalry or race for supremacy as the reason for heated debates and arguments. This rivalry or competition for supremacy of opinion is the core evidence of pride.

Proud people usually refuse to yield grounds; they always want to win every argument or dispute. Proud people are selfish and self-centred. If you examine yourself you will realise that you are selfish, especially when all you see is what that other person does wrong. If you keep pointing fingers at the other person you will not be able to find peace in your relationship.

Pride never admits it's wrong, it always points fingers at others.

To end the conflict in your relationship, you will have to stop pointing fingers and rather start admitting where you are at fault and commit to changing yourself.

The problem with most people in relationship is that they are overtly committed to changing the other person. So, they spend all their time debating about what the other person needs to change instead of focusing on themselves changing.

CONFLICT RESOLUTION

Such people see nothing wrong in their actions, but they pass all the blame on the other person.

Those who even dare to admit that they are at fault only do it in passing but quickly revert to pointing out on the other person's faults.

Do not allow pride to destroy your relationship. Learn to be humble. Humble people admit to their faults, but proud people believe everyone is at fault and they are the only ones right.

Take a close look at your relationship and decide to humble yourself in that relationship. You do not always have to win the argument, allow the other person to win by doing things his or her way. Things do not always have to be done your way.

Just let go of pride and you will see peace returning into that relationship.

I pray that the Holy Spirit will clothe you with the garment of humility in Jesus name.

To resolve any conflict that may be on going in your relationship now do the following.

Firstly, decide to sit down and talk about the situation. Before you start talking take time to pray and take authority over the devil who is the architect of all conflicts and make a commitment to God that as you speak with each other you will do so respectfully.

Listen to each other. Avoid the temptation of jumping in to defend yourself when the other person is still talking. Make commitment to each other to allow each other finish before you respond to what was raised.

Apologise if your spouse highlights what you have done wrong. Apologise first without trying to defend your actions. One common mistake couples make is that they spend time justifying themselves instead of admitting and apologising for the hurt the other person feels.

Learn to accept to be in the wrong even if you are feeling otherwise for peace sake. The scripture commands us to submit one to another in the fear of God.

CHAPTER 10

SUBMISSION THE KINGDOM WAY TO A JOYOUS MARRIAGE

Submitting yourselves one to another in the fear of God.

Wives, submit yourselves unto your own husbands, as unto the Lord.

EPHESIANS 5:21-22

Submission is one of the characteristics of a spirit filled life and key virtue that must be in your life if your relationships will be free from conflicts. God wants every believer to live under the control of the Holy Spirit all the time. When the Holy Spirit is in control of your life. One of the common evidence will be that you will be very submissive. A spirit filled believer will be submitted to God's word by being willing to do whatever God's word says without arguments.

The dictionary meaning of the word submission means; to give over or yield to the power or authority of another. God wants all of us to yield to the power and authority of His word in our daily life.

Jesus demonstrated true submission in relationship by being totally submitted to His father even to the point of death on the cross because He was filled and controlled by the Holy Spirit.

Submission could be very difficult if you are not living a spirit filled life. It is therefore important to spend quality time to pray constantly in order to keep the anointing of the Holy Spirit fresh on your life all the time.

Those who are not born again and have not received the Lordship of Jesus over their lives cannot practice submission God's way, hence the scripture admonishes single people not to marry anyone who is unsaved.

Whenever there is a struggle and unwillingness to be submissive, it is indicative that the concerned persons are not filled with the Holy Spirit and hence are under the influence of Satan through their carnality.

Carnality which manifests primarily in selfishness is the biggest cause for conflicts today.

To be selfish means to be devoted to or caring only for oneself. It means to be concerned primarily with one's own interests regardless of others. A selfish person seeks only his or her own way. Most relationships are facing conflicts today because of selfishness.

Submission is a kingdom requirement from all those in relationship. Husbands and wives are required by God to submit themselves one to another. If you are in a relationship and your relationship has been facing conflicts, then you need to stop and examine yourself.

Ask yourself, *'am I being selfish in this relationship?'* If you can honestly answer that question you will easily identify the root cause of the problem in that relationship.

I encourage you to stop talking about what other people are not doing or are doing and focus on yourself. It is very easy to see a thousand things the other person is not doing right and be totally blinded by selfishness to how selfish you are yourself.

God wants us to live a joyful and happy life. If we do things the way God wants us to, it will lead us into a life full of Joy.

If you are in a relationship which is causing you a lot of pain now, it is possible that Satan has gained access into that relationship subtly.

Selfishness opens the door for Satan to gain access into relationships because selfishness is Satan's way of doing things. God's way is always to be selfless.

I pray for grace to be selfless for you. I call change for good into your relationships in Jesus name.

LET THIS MIND BE IN YOU

Let this mind be in you, which was also in Christ Jesus:

Who, being in the form of God, thought it not robbery to be equal with God:

PHILIPPIANS 2:5-6

A mindset of humility is key to success in relationship. A humble mindset makes it easy for you to be submissive.

Our Lord Jesus did not think it robbery for Him to have to be the one who yields His position as God to become man.

The scripture commands us to submit ourselves one to another. To achieve this, we must never feel like we are being robbed of our rights. Pride is the reason why many people find it difficult to submit. When you are filled with the Holy Spirit you will submit easily.

If you are full of selfishness and all you are concerned with is how to have your way or win in every conversation, then you will struggle with submission.

Do you feel like you are being robbed when you have to submit to someone else?

God commands wives to submit to their husbands because He expects husbands to submit to His word. Husbands before you start demanding submission verbally, examine your life whether you are loving your wife as Christ loved the church and that you are submitted to God's word in your actions towards her.

Wife, every time you say, *'but must I always submit?' What about Him?'* It means that you are thinking it robbery to be submissive and you need to take on Jesus' mindset of humility. Focus on yourself and do not point fingers at what the other person is not doing right. Focus on obeying God.

Jesus also did not consider it as robbery when He had to relinquish the relationship He had with God the Father so that we can become His bride.

Do you feel that your spouse is robbing you of your relationship with your biological family? Certainly, there will still be a relationship between you and your biological family; however, the order of your priority has to change.

Your spouse must come first in the application of your time, resources and attention before your biological parents or siblings.

The scripture says, therefore shall a man leave his father and mother and cleave to his wife. A great deal of people find it difficult to actually leave and cleave as a result they allow their parents or siblings to interfere in their marriage.

Examine your love life today by asking yourself the following questions: Am I selfish or selfless? Do I always want to have things done my way or am I willing to give up my rights to make my partner or friend happy?

What is love to you? Is it about what you can get out of that person or what you are willing to give to that person?

If you say you are in love what exactly do you mean? The implication of being in love is that you are supposed to be willing to give up everything if necessary, to make that person you are in love with happy without feeling robbed.

> Herein is love, not that we loved God, but that he loved us, and sent his Son to be the propitiation for our sins.
>
> 1JOHN 4:10

True love gives love not because of what it can get from you in return but because loving you gives it fulfilment. I pray for the grace to love selflessly in Jesus name.

CHAPTER 11

HOW TO DEAL WITH A DIFFICULT SPOUSE

Likewise, ye wives, be in subjection to your own husbands; that, if any obey not the word, they also may without the word be won by the conversation of the wives;

1Peter 3:1

Submission is a spiritual force which most people have not yet realised. It is a force which the scripture reveals can tame the most difficult person.

Most times believers face issues simply because they try to use other methods other than the one which God has prescribed. In Peter's epistle to the church, he specifically prescribed submission to wives and all those under authority as a medicine for dealing with difficult husbands and leaders.

Did you know that submission can change any leaders attitude towards you?

God commands wives to be in subjection or be submissive to their own husbands. Regardless of whether your husband is obedient to God's word himself or not. If they are disobedient to God's word and you are submissive, then through your lifestyle of submission they will have a change of heart.

If you are a wife, to seek first the kingdom of God means doing the above scripture without asking questions. Before you start trying to bring up all the practical realities you may be facing, first attempt to obey this scripture in its entirety and see whether things will not change.

Most women always say things like, *'my husband is the head, let him lead by example by doing his part.'* God in this scripture says, you should submit even when your husband is not obeying the word; meaning even when he is not showing leadership.

That scripture reveals that your submission will impact on him and change him. This principle is applicable even in the work place. If you have a difficult boss, try being submissive to all his or her instructions and see if there will not be a change.

Someone may say, *'Pastor, I obey my husband and I always do everything he says but he still does not change but rather is taking undue advantage of my submissiveness'.*

Firstly, you must know that in being obedient, it is not just about doing what you are asked to do but doing so with a humble attitude.

A humble attitude must go with your submissiveness. You shouldn't expect results if you obey with a sarcastic attitude. What is your attitude like? Is it a meek attitude or is your attitude rebellious in your outward expressions? Do you frown even though you are obeying, or do you wear a joyful countenance?

Secondly, 1Peter 2:19 says *"For this is thankworthy, if a man for conscience toward God endure grief, suffering wrongfully."*

I encourage you based on above scripture to endure the grief even if you are suffering wrongfully and do not stop being submissive. God will rise to defend you.

For single unmarried ladies, it is important for you to ensure that whoever you go into a relationship with is someone who you would be able to easily submit to.

It is usually easier to be able to submit to a spirit filled man than one who is not spirit filled. Before you say yes to anyone in going into a relationship, ask yourself, *'is he or she filled with the Holy Spirit and living a Spirit controlled life?'*

A person who is not living under the dictates of the Holy Spirit will certainly not make a good husband or wife because such a person will not obey what the Word requires husbands and wives to do.

For all men, it is important to note that submission is not the responsibility of the ladies only. God says submitting yourselves one to another in the fear of God. Message

Translation puts it this way; *Ephesians 5:21 Out of respect for Christ, be courteously reverent to one another.*

Be courteously reverent towards your wife out of respect for Christ and not because she deserves it. You may find yourself in a relationship where your wife is the difficult person. You should avoid the temptation to become violent against her or become physical against her. Respond to her according to the following scripture;

> In meekness instructing those that oppose themselves; if God peradventure will give them repentance to the acknowledging of the truth;
>
> 2Timothy 2:25

This scripture does not say in violence correct your stubborn wife or difficult partner, rather it says in meekness instructing those who oppose themselves; if peradventure God will give them repentance to acknowledge their wrong behaviour. Be meek towards your wife and speak to her respectfully even if she is difficult. When she is calm you can better point out her wrong, and she will be more disposed to changing when she sees that you respect her when she did not deserve it.

I pray for grace for submission for you. I proclaim peace and harmony upon your relationship in Jesus name.

CHAPTER 12

LONGSUFFERING IN RELATIONSHIPS

Put on therefore, as the elect of God, holy and beloved, bowels of mercies, kindness, humbleness of mind, meekness, longsuffering;

Forbearing one another, and forgiving one another, if any man have a quarrel against any: even as Christ forgave you, so also do ye.

COLOSSIANS 3:12-13

I would like to ask you to prepare your mind before you read this chapter. If you are facing a difficult time in your marriage or relationship, an invincible wall of anger may already be in place on your mind that might prevent you from receiving the revelations and instructions that God has for you in this chapter.

Once most people hear the word longsuffering, their first and immediate reaction is how long will I keep suffering?

I admonish you to let down any invincible wall in your mind and read the following with a willingness to do what God's word says regardless of your current circumstances.

Longsuffering is one of the Christian virtues which every believer ought to be walking in. There is very little known about this subject because it is one of those subjects which no one wants to listen to or talk about. Did you know that longsuffering is one of the virtues which God Himself is rich in? Romans 2:4 speaks of the riches of God's goodness, forbearance and longsuffering.

> Or despisest thou the riches of his goodness and forbearance and longsuffering; not knowing that the goodness of God leadeth thee to repentance?
>
> ROMANS 2:4

This scripture reveals to us that God is rich in longsuffering and if that be the case, every believer ought to be rich in longsuffering. The key reason why God is rich in long suffering is because His goodness leads us to repentance. This reveals to us that if you are in a relationship with someone who treats you badly, such a person can be brought to repentance if you endure the ill treatment and rather respond to the person by being good to them.

Goodness exercised over a long period makes people change. The reason for longsuffering is to provide enough room for goodness to finish its work on the person who needs to change.

A lot of people become tired very easily and are hasty to change or jump ship. Most believers do not know how to stay tenaciously in a place or on a vision for a long time. Most people want things to move quickly and if it is not quick they conclude that something must be wrong.

Many believers become tired easily of relationships to the extent they want to change from that relationship and possibly go into a different one. Others get tired of their church not necessarily because the church is a bad church but simply because they just cannot stay for a long time in one place or on a thing. Most people, even believers lack longsuffering. Lack of longsuffering is one reason why many married people decide to go for a divorce.

The Greek word translated 'Longsuffering' in the New Testament is the word 'Macrothumia' and the Thayer's dictionary of Greek words defines that word as patience, endurance, constancy, steadfastness, perseverance, forbearance and slowness in avenging wrongs.

Longsuffering means to endure injury, trouble or provocation for a long time and patiently. Longsuffering means to endure the injury inflicted on you by people around you without you changing your character.

God wants us to be rich in longsuffering and to have a huge shock absorber in our system such that regardless of what people do to you, you are still the same way towards them. Abraham only received the promises of God after he had patiently endured for several years. Longsuffering and endurance are necessary if you will inherit the promise of heaven on earth in your marriage and relationships.

During times of difficulty, the children of Israel could not bear the hardship of the wilderness. At the slightest of obstacle, they threatened to walk away from God's program and plan for their lives.

They wanted to go back to Egypt right from the first day they left. As soon as they saw the Egyptian soldiers matching towards them, they completely cast away their confidence in God. People who do not have the virtue of longsuffering loose hope very easily in God. Some people walk away from churches where God plants them at the slightest of difficulties. Others abandon relationships because they lack longsuffering.

If you are in a relationship, you should not be looking for how to easily abandon it and start another one. If you are married, you should not even allow the thought of divorce rise up in your mind because of what you are going through.

Divorce always starts as a thought, it is important to kill that thought by casting it down from your mind because if you do not do so, the devil will constantly cause it to rise up in your mind and pressure you into it.

How long can you last in the face of provocation? Do you remain consistently constant in faith regardless of the hardship you are surrounded by or do you breakdown and give up very easily?

What is your first response when the going goes tough?

LONGSUFFERING IN RELATIONSHIPS

Do you quit easily, or do you stand your grounds in faith consistently?

Patience simply means consistency. Being consistent in anything you do. Many people are like the man who built his house upon the sand. When the floods came, and the winds blew against the house, the house collapsed because it was founded on the sand. Sand is porous and cannot withstand pressure.

Longsuffering is such an important virtue that Paul described it as one of the true marks of genuine ministers and children of God.

> But in all things approving ourselves as the ministers of God, in much patience, in afflictions, in necessities, in distresses,
>
> By pureness, by knowledge, by longsuffering, by kindness, by the Holy Ghost, by love unfeigned,
>
> 2CORINTHIANS 6:4-6

HOW TO DEVELOP LONGSUFFERING

> For this cause we also, since the day we heard it, do not cease to pray for you, and to desire that ye might be filled with the knowledge of his will in all wisdom and spiritual understanding;
>
> That ye might walk worthy of the Lord unto all pleasing, being fruitful in every good work, and increasing in the knowledge of God;
>
> Strengthened with all might, according to his glorious power, unto all patience and longsuffering with joyfulness;
>
> COLOSSIANS 1:9-11

Paul prayed for the Colossian church a prayer which you need to start praying for yourself and for your spouse if you want to develop the attribute of longsuffering.

He prayed that we might be filled with the knowledge of God's will in wisdom and spiritual understanding. Once you gain insight into the fact that God's will for you while in relationship is to be submissive and to allow the Holy Spirit control you, you will immediately find it easy to endure harsh treatment from your spouse or partner.

You need to pray for yourself and your partner that both of you should walk worthy of the Lord unto all pleasing and be fruitful in every good work and increasing in the knowledge of God.

The more you increase in the knowledge of God, the more you will be gracious in your walk and being gracious will certainly please God.

You also need to pray for yourself and for your spouse to be strengthened with all might unto patience and longsuffering with joyfulness.

The Holy Spirit can strengthen you to be patient and longsuffering, you need to ask for it in prayer. I encourage you to make Colossians 1:9-11 your constant prayer point.

I pray that you will be strengthened with might according to God's glorious power unto all patience and longsuffering with Joyfulness in Jesus name.

CHAPTER 13

COMMUNICATION IN RELATIONSHIP

My beloved is unto me as a cluster of camphire in the vineyards of Engedi.

Behold, thou art fair, my love; behold, thou art fair; thou hast doves' eyes.

Behold, thou art fair, my beloved, yea, pleasant: also our bed is green.

SONGS OF SOLOMON 1:14-16

Communication is the heart and life of any relationship. Love cannot exist between any two people except it is first expressed through words. To sustain the love in your relationship it is important to constantly communicate with your spouse or partner.

THE ART OF COMMUNICATION

Communication in any relationship is an art which everyone in relationship must learn. This is so because no two relationships are the same because of the different character traits that everyone in relationship possesses. For effective communication to exist in your relationship, you must understand the peculiar traits of who you are dealing with.

Some people are slow to comprehend things whereas others are not slow. Some people hate the use of certain words whereas others were raised in environments where such words are used freely. It is therefore necessary to contextualise your communication skills to the peculiar traits of your partner. The secret is to identify what works and stick to it.

IMPORTANCE OF COMMUNICATION

Why is it important to communicate freely about everything in your marriage or relationship? A proper understanding of the importance of communication will make you give proper attention to it.

People usually take things that are of value to them seriously, once you understand the importance of communication, you will start doing your best to ensure that effective communication is constantly taking place between you and your spouse as well as those with whom you are in relationship.

Let's look at a few reasons why it is important to communicate effectively in your relationship.

COMMUNICATION IN RELATIONSHIP

COMMUNICATION CONTROLS THE HEALTH OF YOUR RELATIONSHIP

You can ascertain the health of your relationship by analysing how easily and freely you and your spouse or partner communicate about everything.

If communication breaks down, everything else in that relationship will break down.

COMMUNICATION CREATES INFORMATION FLOW

Information is very critical in all our decision-making processes. Without proper information flow no relationship can become what the participants desire. This is one of the key reasons why it is important to communicate.

You should never be in a situation where you and your spouse are on an outing and you say something in public and your spouse responds by saying, '*I never knew that*', or '*how come you never told me?*' This would certainly be very embarrassing for both of you.

Your partner will not know what is going on in your life if you do not communicate with him or her. You cannot be in a relationship where you and your partner never engage on anything. You must engage and relate on a wide variety of issues and these engagements depend on effective information flow to exist.

COMMUNICATION HELPS IN DECISION MAKING

Information is the key to making right or wrong decisions. When you communicate your opinion to your spouse during times of decision making, it helps your spouse to avoid decisions that could hurt you or hurt the family.

For those who are single, it is critically important to communicate openly because you need to know exactly what you are going into before you agree to marry someone.

It would be deceptive of you if you withhold important information from someone you claim to love who may have changed his or her mind about you if they knew something you did not disclose.

If you do that it simply means that you deceived the person into that relationship and sooner or later the truth will be revealed.

It is better to reveal the truth and let the person make an informed decision even if it will lead to you losing out.

COMMUNICATION HELPS TO BREED UNDERSTANDING BETWEEN COUPLES

One of the biggest challenges that some couples face is the inability to understand themselves and the reasons behind certain behaviours being exhibited. People's actions in their relationships are based on ideas and thoughts they have on their minds and if they fail to communicate these ideas, the other party finds himself dealing with a character that he does not really understand.

COMMUNICATION HELPS TO CREATE TRUST

Trust is one of the biggest words amongst people in relationship. You hear things like, *'I do not trust him, I cannot trust her.'*

COMMUNICATION IN RELATIONSHIP

The foundation for trust in any relationship is openness and free communication about every subject matter. A situation where married people use passwords on their phones, and computers, denying their spouses access to information on those gadgets certainly creates room for distrust.

In marriage, you should not have any 'skeletons in your cupboards'. If you do, you have already provided for failure in that relationship.

If you have nothing to hide, then you should give your partner open access to every aspect of your life including your phones, laptops and computers.

There should be no secret between the two of you!

There are tremendous benefits of openness. If you are an open person, you plug the holes for you to fall into temptations. One reason why people end up cheating is because they have all these secrets and so when the temptation for cheating comes to them, they easily fall and it becomes a part of their numerous secrets which ultimately hurts those who they claim to love.

If you do not plan to cheat against your partner, then you should be open and plain constantly about every subject matter.

COMMUNICATION HELPS YOU TO BECOME ONE

Therefore shall a man leave his father and his mother, and shall cleave unto his wife: and they shall be one flesh.

And they were both naked, the man and his wife, and were not ashamed.

GENESIS 2:24-25

God planned for people in relationship to become one flesh. Adam and Eve were both naked and not ashamed because they had all things common.

Marriage is a call to oneness. You must be willing to share oneness in every area. You cannot have areas of your life which are secretive.

Secretiveness kills oneness. To achieve this you must be selfless. Selfishness is the reason why many people are not open to their spouses.

WHAT YOU SHOULD COMMUNICATE ABOUT

TALK ABOUT YOUR PAST: Your past relationships, hurts failures, things that you are not proud about. Do not hide anything from your spouse or partner.

I know someone may be saying, *'is it necessary to talk about everything?'* The fact is that who you are today, your behaviours and the way you act are influenced by your past experiences.

If you fail or refuse to talk about your past with your spouse or partner you create room for the devil to use that past to bring down your relationship because everything hidden always comes into public view and when something you hid from your partner comes into view, your partner will lose all trust he or she ever had in you prior to that time.

COMMUNICATION IN RELATIONSHIP

TALK ABOUT YOUR WEAKNESSES: Let there be no surprises in your relationship. If you are struggling with a weakness in your life, it is important to disclose it fully to your partner.

> Two *are* better than one; because they have a good reward for their labour.
>
> For if they fall, the one will lift up his fellow: but woe to him *that is* alone when he falleth; for *he hath* not another to help him up.
>
> Again, if two lie together, then they have heat: but how can one be warm *alone*?
>
> ECCLESIASTES 4:9-11

The scripture declares that two are better than one; if they fall the one will lift the other up, but woe unto him that is alone when he falls. You and your partner can better work to overcome your weakness if you disclose it than if you try to fix things alone.

TALK ABOUT SEX: Talk about your sex life, what you like and what you do not like. Never assume that your spouse knows how to make love to you. You are different, you need to help him or her satisfy you by communicating what you like. Talk about you past sex life, if you were abused or hyper active sexually in the past, your spouse needs to know because these past experiences influence your behaviour now so be fully transparent.

TALK ABOUT YOUR FINANCES: Your spouse should have access to your financial information and both of you should work on openness with regards to financial dealings. Communicate before you do anything new or anything that is not within your normal daily or weekly routine.

COMMON REASONS WHY PEOPLE CONCEAL INFORMATION

Hiding anything from your partner is an indication of lack of trust which on its own could damage your relationship further if it is already troubled. You build trust by being transparent not by hiding information.

Sometimes out of fear of how the other party would react to the information, people in relationship choose to hide things. You need to know that it is better to be crucified for being honest and transparent than to resort to hiding things from your spouse as a result of fear. Chose to be transparent regardless of what it will cost you. The truth once it is in the open always sets anyone free.

If your spouse or partner discloses information to you avoid being judgmental. Once you do not crucify them, next time it will be easy for them to tell you more things. Some people hide things because of the fear of being stopped from taking an action or step they want to take. If you hide things for this reason it reflects selfishness on your part.

You must be willing to subject your choices or decisions to scrutiny. If you believe your decision is good, then defend it before your spouse or partner. Two heads are better than one. Unilateral action will always hurt your relationship.

EFFECTIVE COMMUNICATION SKILLS

RIGHT TIMING: You need to consider right timing if you want to develop an effective communication with your partner. If

COMMUNICATION IN RELATIONSHIP

your spouse is given to sports for example and you know that he or she is consumed at that time, it would be wise to wait for a better time before you start bringing up domestic issues.

Wrong timing in communication can cause you not to receive the same kind of response you would desire from your spouse or partner.

MEASURE CONSTANTLY: Measure the mood of your spouse or partner. Be wise! Only start a conversation when the mood is right. Avoid trying to bring correction when the atmosphere is already tense. While holding a conversation, measure continuously the effect of your words as you speak. Many times, people get hurt by those who love them because they do not measure the impact of their words. Choose your words carefully when you speak. You could do a lot of damage if you use the wrong words whereas speaking the right words could do a lot of good.

WHAT YOU SAID VERSUS WHAT YOU MEAN: Several times people in relationship say something different from what they mean, and they expect their partners to respond to what they mean but what they said is directly opposite to what they mean.

Examine what you say constantly and be sure it is a true reflection of what you meant to say. If you are not clear, seek clarity and never assume a meaning to what was said if you are not sure.

THE POWER OF SILENCE: One of the tools to deploy to achieve lasting peace is the power of silence. Some men think that being the head of the home implies that they must always say something all the time. Experience has shown that you can actually say a lot through silence. Learn when to be quiet.

WHAT COMMUNICATION IS NOT

COMPLAINING: Complaining is not an acceptable way of communicating in a relationship. Complaining is being critical and nagging. It is expressing a known displeasure in a negative way. When you complain, you attack your partner and that will not yield your desired results.

SHOUTING: Shouting is another unacceptable way of communicating in relationship. When you shout, both of you do not hear yourselves and you end up hurting each other. Shouting is a demonstration of a weakness and a reflection of inability to manage your emotions. You are saying publicly by shouting that you are weak emotionally and unable to control your anger. Avoid shouting at your partner regardless of the provocation.

MURMURING: Murmuring is speaking under your breath in a nagging way. It is speaking either to oneself or to a second party in such a way that the object does not hear.

SPEAKING WITH INTENT TO HURT: Never communicate with intention to hurt. Some people in relationship plan the use of their words and chose what to say primarily because they want to hurt the other person and they know what to say to inflict hurt. That is wickedness and as a Christian you should not hurt anyone you love deliberately. Avoid the temptation to retaliate when you hurt because the scripture commands you not to repay evil for evil but to overcome evil with good.

COMMUNICATION IN RELATIONSHIP

INITIATING COMMUNICATION

The key to initiating communication is questioning everything. Questions provide room for answers especially when the party concerned does not proffer information voluntarily.

If you are married, it is important to keep in mind that you will be questioned for decisions and actions which while you were a single man or woman you took without anyone questioning you. Most married people still want to live and act as though they are still single and unmarried. You must adapt your mind to the reality that you are now married and as a married man or woman you must communicate about every action before you take them and after you take them. You must be willing to subject yourself to scrutiny for the health of your relationship. You lost your right to privacy the day you decided to get married.

Many times, people in relationship do not want to talk about certain things for different reasons. The responsibility then falls upon the one who needs the information being withheld to ask questions.

A great deal of people kill communication by saying, *'I do not want to talk about that.'* If you are in the game of doing this, you need to know that this attitude hurts the health of your relationship.

It is worth noting that regardless of your reasons for not wanting to discuss the subject matter, you owe it to the person you claim to love to be fully transparent because a failure to be fully transparent is simply being deceptive and your relationship will develop cracks as a result.

Fear is always at the root of holding back on information and you need to deal with your fears. Where necessary seek assurances from the person involved that they would not use such information you are withholding to form wrong opinions about you and then open up.

If you are unmarried and are refusing to discuss certain aspects of your life with someone you are trying to build a future with, then you are being unwise and laying a foundation which will come back to hurt the relationship if it does go on.

I encourage all single people never to accept the excuse of not wanting to talk about a particular subject matter from anyone who claims to be in love with you. If he or she loves you, then there must be proof, and the proof of love is giving all and holding nothing back. God so loved us that he gave us his all.

Therefore, let no man glory in men. For all things are yours;

Whether Paul, or Apollos, or Cephas, or the world, or life, or death, or things present, or things to come; all are yours;

And ye are Christ's; and Christ is God's.

1 CORINTHIANS 3:21

God has given us his all because of his love. The scripture declares that all things are ours. He did not hold back anything from us. We should all seek to act like our God.

CHAPTER 14

HARVESTING HONEY FROM YOUR HONEY PRODUCER

And they told him, and said, We came unto the land whither thou sentest us, and surely it floweth with milk and honey; and this is the fruit of it.

NUMBER 13:27

In this chapter, I would like to draw your attention to how you can harvest honey out of your 'honey producer'!

The term Honey is mostly used as a pet name for our spouses. Most of us use that word without taking time to examine the source of honey in the natural. There are several lessons to be learnt about relationships from the life of a Bee.

A bee is an insect which could be very deadly because of its sting. Every Honeybee has capacity to produce honey;

however, to reap honey out of the Bee you must understand certain things about the Bee and with such knowledge know how to manage the Bee.

In every wife or husband is the good and sweet side; and just like the Bee there is also the part of most people that is like the sting of the Bee.

This sting part is the reason why there are conflicts in many marriages. Some people feel like all they get out of their spouse is the Bee sting rather than the honey.

To harvest 'honey' out of your spouse, do the following.

RECOGNIZE THAT THERE IS NO PERFECT PERSON

Your spouse has a 'bee-ish' sting which sometimes shows up. This 'bee-ish' sting does not imply that you are in a wrong relationship. It only implies that you have not gained the necessary knowledge of how to manage him or her in that relationship, so that you can reap the honey.

The fact that a Bee stings does not mean that it does not produce honey.

FOCUS ON THE HONEY NOT THE STING

The reason why anyone would engage in Bee farming is because they focus on the honey rather than the sting of a bee. If you want honey, you need to be aware that only Bees produce them, and Bees had a sting. You cannot have a Bee without the sting.

The lesson here is that you must focus on the strengths of that person you are in a relationship with while adapting yourself to manage the weaknesses of that person because like the Bee you cannot have a person's good sides without having to deal with his bad sides.

Verbally recognize and praise the strengths of your partner while lovingly encouraging adjustments where adjustments need to be made.

Avoid criticizing and picking on the faults of your partner. When you point fingers and constantly talk about the faults and inadequacies of your partner you will aggravate the person and you might get a Bee sting rather than the honey you desire.

BE WILLING TO UNDERTAKE THE WORK REQUIRED

To make a relationship work, you must be willing like the Bee farmers to undertake the work required before you can harvest Honey. Relationships need some work to be done to make it work. Discover what brings out the Bee sting out of your spouse or partner and endeavour to avoid doing such. Bees sting when aggravated. Avoid being a source of aggravation to your partner.

UNDERSTANDING THE HONEY-BEE CONCEPT IN RELATIONSHIPS

A soft answer turneth away wrath: but grievous words stir up anger.

PROVERBS 15:1

Bee farmers know that they must put on a beekeeping suit when going to harvest honey from the beehive, this costume is usually made of an impregnable fabric.

HEAVEN ON EARTH IN MARRIAGE & RELATIONSHIPS

The Bee will naturally sting when agitated or aggravated and hence the antidote is not trying to change the nature of the Bee from stinging but rather protecting yourself and ensuring that your reactions are managed.

In relationships, we call our spouses honey because of the sweetness we derive in being in love with them but there are sides of each person that passes for the Bee sting of a honey Bee.

The same way a Bee farmer deals with the Bee to harvest Honey out of it, is the same principle we must apply to our relationships in order to derive Joy from it.

To harvest honey, you must remain calm and focused on the honey you are harvesting as earlier mentioned. If a Bee finds its way into your under clothing and stings you, your reaction must be controlled. You do not want to stir up an avalanche of Bee attack by overreacting.

In marriage one common error that occurs is the fact that couples are busy trying to get their partners to change.

Your spouse is your honey producer and just like the Bee that produces honey, they also have those undesired sharp edges that passes for a Bee sting.

The right approach in dealing with your honey producer is to adapt to the reality of the sting which exists in the honey producer by putting on the protective garment of HUMILITY, SELFLESSNESS AND GRACE. And choosing not to react to further agitate or aggravate the Bee to sting more. FOCUS ON YOUR REACTION!

Be a loving Christian in your relationship. Do not change your character because of the actions of your partner. Love always wins! You will discover that the most difficult person will begin to soften up and change when they experience true love.

Anger always precedes every aggressive action of your spouse or partner which passes for a Bee sting.

"A soft answer turneth away wrath: but grievous words stir up anger.

The tongue of the wise useth knowledge aright: but the mouth of fools poureth out foolishness."

PROVERBS 15:1-2

One principal way to quell the heat of anger is found here. A soft answer turns away wrath or anger! Wise people use their tongue properly to quell the heat of anger when it rises.

Bees usually sting when you stir or agitate their beehive. In relationship answering softly when your partner is angry will calm his or her nerves.

Anger is not a propriety of nobles. I encourage you to deal with anger in your life if you are used to always getting angry. Anger is a sign of great weakness, it is indicative of the fact that you cannot control your emotions.

CHAPTER 15

WHAT MEN & WOMEN WANT FROM THEIR SPOUSES

Likewise, ye husbands, dwell with them according to knowledge, giving honour unto the wife, as unto the weaker vessel, and as being heirs together of the grace of life; that your prayers be not hindered.

1PETER 3:7

WHAT MEN WANT

We live in a day when many are clamouring for gender equality. However, It is important for us not to misplace our values in the midst of it all. The man was made by God to be the head of his home and it is important for wives to understand that God expects them to respect and honour their husbands in that God given position.

Even when your husband has acted disrespectfully or out of line, God's expectations of you doesn't change, do not fall into the temptation of using his actions as a licence to usurp authority or to disrespect him in return. Learn to hold back because you recognise that he is in authority above you.

MEN DO NOT LIKE WOMEN ARGUING WITH THEM

Men do not like women who argue with them continuously. It always comes out as though you are competing with them for their position as the head of the home. Argumentativeness in your relationship is not a way to prove your worth or relevance. God commands you to be meek; and meekness is not a reflection of weakness but rather it is a demonstration of maturity in controlling your emotions and actions.

Most men love their wives to be meek towards them.

MEN DO NOT LIKE NAGGING WOMEN

There are many ladies who specialise in nagging and complaining about what their husbands are not doing right and so on. The truth is that you will end up turning your husband off towards you and he would not want to come home to be with you because you are always nagging at him. Nagging always yields a negative result.

MEN DO NOT LIKE SEXUALLY PASSIVE WOMEN

Most ladies pride in the fact that they can do without sex for a long time and they forget that the chemistry of a man is different from that of a woman. While you may be able to abstain from sex for a long time, your husband needs to be satisfied. You must go out of your way to please him sexually.

Also, while making love, men like their wives to be active and to initiate sex. They also like women that are aggressive and adventurous rather than boring women.

Most ladies always make excuses when it comes to love making with their husbands. They make excuses like, *'I am tired, I am not in the mood and so on.'*

The scripture says that the woman has no power over her body but the man and vice versa. In Paul's writing to the Corinthians he warned believers not to defraud one another by starving each other of sex, except it be by consent that you may seek the Lord for a specific length of time.

> Defraud ye not one the other, except *it be* with consent for a time, that ye may give yourselves to fasting and prayer; and come together again, that Satan tempt you not for your incontinency.
>
> 1CORINTIANS 7:5

According to Paul's writing above, If you starve your spouse of sex, you are committing fraud!

WHAT WOMEN WANT FROM THEIR HUSBANDS

Most men are always so busy they hardly spend time with their wives. This was the problem that Adam suffered from. He was not spending time with his wife and hence the snake got a chance to creep in on his wife to fill the gap. Whoever is spending more time with your wife is moulding her.

Invest time into being with your wife. You cannot become so overwhelmed with working that your relationship with your wife suffers.

COMPLEMENT THEM

A woman wants to feel attractive to her husband and wants to know she is meeting up to the expectations of her spouse. It is important to complement her. Complement her looks and avoid the temptation of saying things as you see it. If she is not looking as good as you would want, use a positive way to encourage her to improve

on her looks.

Most men are so critical that they kill the spirit of their spouses. When she has made an effort to look good, do not wait for her to ask you how she looks before you say something.

REASSURE HER CONSTANTLY OF YOUR LOVE

Tell your wife constantly that you love her by your words and actions. Women want their husbands to constantly reassure them of their love. Never assume that your wife knows you love her without you reassuring her.

BE SENSITIVE

Women want their husbands to be sensitive to what they go through. Be sensitive to the emotional swings that comes into place when she is going through her menstrual circle.

WHAT MEN & WOMEN WANT FROM THEIR SPOUSES

Sometimes your wife may become overwhelmed with caring for the kids and also caring for you that she may become emotionally drained.

Be sensitive and lend a helping hand where possible to relieve her pressure domestically. You can help out in the kitchen or help out with caring for the children.

PROTECT THEM

Women want to feel safe and protected by their husbands. In times of conflicts with third parties learn to stand up and defend your wife publicly even if she is wrong. You can correct her privately but first protect and defend her publicly.

MAKE THEM KNOW THAT THEY ARE THE NUMBER ONE IN YOUR LIFE

Women want to know that aside from God they are the number one in your life. It is important to ensure that you give this impression clearly especially when it comes to dealing with your immediate family. Many men put their immediate family above their wife and that hurts their relationship with their wife.

WOMEN WANT TO KNOW THAT THEIR HUSBANDS ARE PROUD OF THEM PUBLICLY

Many men subtly create problems for themselves because they do not publicly make it clear that they are married and that they are proud of their spouse.

Celebrate your wife publicly, as you do it will help her to gain more confidence in herself.

CHAPTER 16

THE MAN, FATHER, HUSBAND & LEADER

For the husband is the head of the wife, even as Christ is the head of the church: and he is the saviour of the body.

Husbands, love your wives, even as Christ also loved the church, and gave himself for it;

EPHESIANS 5:23, 25

Our Lord Jesus Christ, in his care, love, and affection for the church, perfectly exemplifies God's expectations regarding the responsibilities of a man to his family.

Just as Christ Jesus is the head, the leader, the husband, the father and high priest of the church so also every man has been called to fulfil a multifaceted ministry to his family.

Fatherhood is a call to leadership; spiritually, morally and in every ramification of life. Love is the governing force of Christ's headship over the church and must also be the driving force behind every man's actions. Love in its truest form is sacrificial. It makes a man become a servant leader over his house. A servant leader is that leader who leads by serving those whom he leads. Christ so loved the world that he gave himself for it and men ought to love their wives and children that way.

In order to be the man, the father, the husband and the leader God wants you to be, you must be willing to sacrifice all; your time, your dreams, your pride etc, so that your spouse and children can have the kind of life God desires for them.

It is impossible to achieve this without a vibrant relationship with the Holy Spirit. One key secret to Christ's love for us is that He maintained a constant relationship with His heavenly father; drawing strength and inspiration from God the father especially during his times of temptations.

Then answered Jesus and said unto them, Verily, verily, I say unto you, The Son can do nothing of himself, but what he seeth the Father do: for what things soever he doeth, these also doeth the Son likewise.

John 5:19

Our Lord Jesus revealed in the above scripture the secret of His success as a man, a father and husband of the church; He said, the Son can do nothing of himself! He watches His father and listens for His directives before He acts.

If you will succeed at your role as a man, husband, father and leader of your family, you must walk in the steps of Jesus. Give attention to your prayer and fellowship time and endeavour to constantly hear from God the father before you do anything.

Your spiritual leadership is defined by your personal relationship with God and your family will generally follow in your footsteps.

To provide good spiritual leadership you must have a good and vibrant prayer life.

THE LEADER AND THE PRINCIPLE OF SELF-CONTROL

As a leader over your family you must exercise the principle of self-control.

Have you ever stopped to think about how self-controlled our Lord Jesus Christ is? Several times we do things that provoke Him, but He never responds in anger towards us.

To lead like Jesus, you must control your temperament and never allow it run wild. You must control your actions, always weighing them in the light of God's word. Control the use of your tongue. Great leaders talk less and act more.

The mouth is not meant for abuses but for putting the blessing on your family. Watch the words you use when communicating with your wife and children.

Control your appetite for things. Man shall not live by bread alone, and godliness with contentment is great gain.

Moderation is a virtue which you must imbibe. Prosperity is good, but its purpose is not for an endless gratification of man's insatiable appetite. Your resources can make better kingdom impact if put into the gospel than buying canal things which perish with use. Lead your family by using your resources for the furtherance of the course of the kingdom of God.

Control your sexual passions, too much of anything is bad. Excessiveness of any kind is unhealthy. Let your moderation be known to all men.

> Let your moderation be known unto all men. The Lord *is* at hand.
>
> PHILIPPIANS 4:5

INTEGRITY AND HONESTY, THE BUILDING BLOCKS OF THE MAN

> But speaking the truth in love, may grow up into him in all things, which is the head, *even* Christ:
>
> EPHESIANS 4:15

Integrity and honesty are fundamental building blocks that ought to be in the life of every man. In Paul's writing to the Ephesians, he revealed that anyone who desires to be like Christ Jesus and to function in the same headship role as Him, must learn to speak the truth in love.

Truthfulness is simply honesty. It is a virtue that defines your inner strength. Lying is a reflection of inner weakness. A lot of men lie a lot to their spouses without knowing that practicing a lying lifestyle weakens their headship and prevents them from growing up into Christlikeness.

THE MAN, HUSBAND, FATHER & LEADER

I motivate you to make a commitment to be honest to your spouse even if you feel she may crucify you for your honesty. Tell her the truth always and refuse the temptation to hide things from her.

Being a man of Integrity means following moral or ethical standards and choosing to do the right thing in all circumstances, even if no one is sees you. Having integrity means to be true to yourself and to do nothing that demeans or dishonours you.

Living a life of integrity means not living a double standard life. Your wife should not stumble into any surprises about you.

A failure to commit to a life of integrity is the reason why some men end up cheating on their wives by having an affair. If you tend to hide things from your wife, you will be more prone to falling into adultery.

A man can hire a prostitute for the price of a loaf of bread, but adultery will cost him all he has. GOOD NEWS TRANSLATION

Proverbs 6:26

THE PRIEST

Now the serpent was more subtil than any beast of the field which the LORD God had made. And he said unto the woman, Yea, hath God said, Ye shall not eat of every tree of the garden?

And the woman said unto the serpent, We may eat of the fruit of the trees of the garden:

GENESIS 3:1-2

As the head of the home, a man has the responsibility of determining the spiritual climate of his household.

In the account of Adam and Eve's fall in the garden of Eden, we see that Adam neglected the critical role of providing spiritual direction to his family.

Eve made the decision for the family to eat the fruit God had told them not to eat and Adam simply followed her footsteps instead of being the leader in the home on spiritual things.

As the priest of over your family, God expects you to take the lead in spiritual matters. Do not leave the responsibility of determining the direction of your family spiritually to your wife. Perhaps the whole world would not have fallen into the hands of Satan, If Adam had done his Job of providing proper spiritual guidance to his family.

It is important for you to invest time to develop yourself spiritual by taking interest in the things of God for you to be able to serve as a priest over your family.

One reason why many ladies end up becoming the priest and spiritual leader in their marriages is because their men do not take interest in the things of God. They do not go to church regularly and as a result find themselves lagging behind in spiritual growth.

Be a different man! Be the man who loves the house of God and who makes time for the things of God. King David in scripture excelled as King because he loved God's house. We know this from his psalm below;

THE MAN, HUSBAND, FATHER & LEADER

> I was glad when they said unto me, Let us go into the house of the LORD.
>
> Psalm 122:1

David loved God's house and even declared that those who love Jerusalem (which was the city of God) shall prosper because of their love for the city.

Lead your family to commit time to serving God by participating in your local church. At home lead your family into a deeper relationship with God by both motivating them and showing them a good example.

As the priest over your family, you are also the shepherd of your home. You must monitor what your wife and children are exposed to. Adam allowed his wife to hang out with a snake and he paid dearly for his laxity.

Women were made for companionship; it is important for you to make time constantly to be with your wife because if you are always an absent father and husband you may end up finding your wife hanging out with allegoric snakes.

LESSONS FROM MR TIMAEUS

> And they came to Jericho: and as he went out of Jericho with his disciples and a great number of people, blind Bartimaeus, the son of Timaeus, sat by the highway side begging.
>
> MARK 10:46

We have a story in the bible about a man by the name of Timaeus who had a son called Blind Bartimaeus. We do not really know the actual name of his son as the Greek word Bartimaeus simply means Son of Timaeus.

This blind Bartimaeus ended up becoming a beggar who sat on a highway begging for survival. We know from the location where he sat begging that he was not a natural beggar but had become a circumstantial beggar because true beggars do not beg on a highway.

His father Timaeus was supposed to be a man of honour but alas he was an absent father! The meaning of the word Timaeus in the Greek is the word honourable. I believe that this blind son of an honourable man became a beggar primarily because though his father's name revealed that he was supposed to be a man of honour, yet there was no record of the whereabouts of his father while his son turned into a beggar.

Mr Timaeus was an absent father and as a result his son became blind and begged on the streets. There is nothing that could be more demeaning than for you as a man to be perceived in your workplace as a man of honour and to be so consumed with your career only for your wife and children to suffer because of neglect of your family responsibilities.

Do not get so busy that you do not have time to pay attention to what your children are developing into. Avoid the trap of outsourcing the training and development of your children to minders and care givers. You must make time for your family.

I believe that Mr Timaeus was absent from the presence of God, absent from commitment to working in God's house, absent from his local church and absent from his duties as a

THE MAN, HUSBAND, FATHER & LEADER

father. He may have been also ignorant of his duties as a husband like most men today who leave the caring of the children solely to their wives without making time to help their children develop.

When Blind Bartimaeus went into begging, we have no record that there was any one there to stop him from going on such an ignoble path. Perhaps Mr Timaeus was the type of man who was tolerant to abnormal developmental tendencies and unable to bring correction to his family As man you must not be tolerant or permissive of wrong behaviour exhibited by members of your household, but rather bring discipline into the lives of your children with love.

You as a father has the responsibility to give vision to your family or else they may end up blinded and become beggars in life. A great deal of wrong behaviour that children exhibit arises because no one gave them a vision to preoccupy them and direct their energy in the right direction. Children are full of energy and this energy must be directed towards meaningful ventures.

A failure to give vision to his family brought shame to Mr Timaeus as people referred to him in talking about his son as they called him Bartimaeus or Son of Timaeus.

XRAY ON ABRAHAM

For I know him, that he will command his children and his household after him, and they shall keep the way of the LORD, to do justice and judgment; that the LORD may bring upon Abraham that which he hath spoken of him.

GENESIS 18:19

In direct contrast to Mr Timaeus, Abraham was a man who brought great leadership and governance to his family.

God gave credence to Abraham's mastery over his household when He said, I know that Abraham will command his children and his household to keep the way of the Lord.

And the LORD said, Shall I hide from Abraham that thing which I do;

Seeing that Abraham shall surely become a great and mighty nation, and all the nations of the earth shall be blessed in him? For I know him, that he will command his children and his household after him, and they shall keep the way of the LORD, to do justice and judgment; that the LORD may bring upon Abraham that which he hath spoken of him.

GENESIS 18:17-19

God acknowledged that Abraham had good oversight over his house and could command his children and ensure that they went in the path of justice and judgement. This reveals to us that every man is responsible for what his children become in life.

Abraham was a man of faith and we see that his son Isaac, his nephew Lot, his wife Sarah all followed his footstep of faith. A key calling of every man is to teach his family how to live by faith. You should not be the doubter in your house. Faith comes by hearing, hearing by the word of God.

THE MAN, HUSBAND, FATHER & LEADER

ABRAHAM WAS A TRAINER

And when Abram heard that his brother was taken captive, he armed his trained servants, born in his own house, three hundred and eighteen, and pursued them unto Dan.

GENESIS 14:14

Abraham had 318 trained men in his house. When Lot his nephew was captured, he used the trained servants in his house as soldiers and went to war with them, securing the release of Lot by defeating his abductors.

A key lesson to learn from him is the fact that every man should seek to train and equip his family members with skills which can be called upon at a time of need.

Train your children on how to do the things you can do so that when you are absent or if the need arises they can carry out the required tasks just like you would.

It is your responsibility as the father to ensure that your children and family also know how to fight for what they believe in. Abraham was a fighter hence he could lead the battle to deliver Lot. He was not a man who gives up easily, we must train our families in that same way.

ABRAHAM WAS DEVOTED TO GOD

Then Abram removed his tent, and came and dwelt in the plain of Mamre, which is in Hebron, and built there an altar unto the LORD.

GENESIS 13:18

Abraham was committed in his walk with God and had a personal relationship with Him. He built altars and worshipped God several times. He was devoted to fellowship with God and made decisions that helped strengthen his walk with God.

> By faith Abraham, when he was called to go out into a place which he should after receive for an inheritance, obeyed; and he went out, not knowing whither he went.
>
> HEBREWS 11:8

Abraham walked in obedience to God's instructions and was willing to leave his country and his father's house when God commanded him to do so even though he did not have a clear picture of where he was moving to.

He was a man of faith. Faith is simply taking God's word and acting upon it.

Abraham was also devoted to God in his finances and depended on God for his prosperity.

> And blessed be the most high God, which hath delivered thine enemies into thy hand. And he gave him tithes of all.
>
> GENESIS 14:20

Abraham was a Tither as seen from Genesis 14:20 when he met Melchizedek after the victory he gained in battle over the kings that abducted his Nephew. He recognised heaven's value systems and taught his family the principle of tithing.

Jacob later vowed to God that he would offer his tithe to Him if He prospered him because he learnt from Abraham

THE MAN, HUSBAND, FATHER & LEADER

and Isaac (His grandfather and father) that honouring God with the tithes is the right way of responding to God's blessings.

As the head of your family you must teach your children godly principles like the principle of tithing and giving in general.

And Jacob vowed a vow, saying, If God will be with me, and will keep me in this way that I go, and will give me bread to eat, and raiment to put on,

So that I come again to my father's house in peace; then shall the LORD be my God:

And this stone, which I have set *for* a pillar, shall be God's house: and of all that thou shalt give me I will surely give the tenth unto thee.

GENESIS 28:20-22

ABRAHAM WAS A MAN OF FINANCIAL INTEGRITY

And Abram said to the king of Sodom, I have lift up mine hand unto the LORD, the most high God, the possessor of heaven and earth,

That I will not *take* from a thread even to a shoe latchet, and that I will not take any thing that *is* thine, lest thou shouldest say, I have made Abram rich:

GENESIS 14:22-23

Abraham was a man of financial probity. He said to the king of Sodom I will not take anything that belongs to you. Even though he had an opportunity to enrich himself through the recovered goods that belonged to the king of Sodom, he did not do so. Having fought the war and won the average person would not act like Abraham did. We learn from him not to seek to enrich ourselves by all means especially when it will hurt somebody else or take undue advantage of somebody's handicap.

HE WAS A PEACE MAKER

> And Abraham took sheep and oxen, and gave them unto Abimelech; and both of them made a covenant.
>
> GENESIS 21:27

Abraham was a peace maker. He avoided strife with Lot and entered into covenants of peace with his host communities.

ESTABLISH THE FOUNDATION FOR A GODLY VALUE SYSTEM

Respect: Train your children and family members to be respectful. Be exemplary by showing respect to your wife especially in the presence of your children. In dealing with your children themselves learn to treat them with respect.

Honour: Honour all men. The proof of honour is respect. Train your family to walk in dignity and honour.

Financial Propriety: Do not accept gifts for favours. Do not misappropriate funds trusted into your care by diverting it. Avoid borrowing because the borrower is always a servant to the lender. Godliness with contentment is great gain. Having food and raiment there with be content. Be content with your wages. Work hard and show your children an example of the reward of working hard.

CHAPTER 17

GOD'S INSTRUCTION TO HUSBANDS

Likewise, ye husbands, dwell with them according to knowledge, giving honour unto the wife, as unto the weaker vessel, and as being heirs together of the grace of life; that your prayers be not hindered.

1PETER 3:7

Husbands, God commands you to dwell with your wives according to knowledge. Take time to know what type of wife you are married to and relate with her according to her personality and needs.

One mistake that most men make is the fact that they presume and act on their presumption on what they think are the needs of their wives. Some men relate with their wives based on how their father used to treat their mother.

You cannot treat or relate with your wife like you relate with your mother, your wife is unique and hence you need to take time to know her specific needs. To gain this knowledge, you have to ask her questions and communicate with her constantly.

Your goal as a husband should be to have a happy wife, if your wife is sad and depressed, your whole family will be filled with gloominess.

You need to know how women communicate to be able to relate with them appropriately. The average woman communicates in a remarkably interesting way. When their countenance is down, and you ask them, *'how are you',* you may get a sharp answer like *'I am fine'.*

You need to immediately know that something is wrong. Go an extra mile to patiently get her to tell you what is wrong. Do not just leave her because she said she was fine.

Women generally want the attention of their husbands; they love it when you show concern for things that matter to them. They are very responsive in nature. Women were made for companionship that is the reason why you find a lot of ladies complaining about their absent husbands.

If you are a busy man, you need to learn the art of constant communication in the midst of your busy schedule. Your spouse knows that you are busy, all they seek for, is for you to have enough regard for their needs to carry them along through constant communication within your busy schedules. Also, when you are not busy endeavour to give them attention.

GOD'S INSTRUCTION TO HUSBANDS

Your wife should come first before your Job, your job is important because it provides for your family however you should always give honour to your wife above the value you give to your Job. You can always get another job but it may be difficult to find another wife who is as good as the one you have now.

God commands you to honour your wife. One key attribute of honour is respect. God commands you to respect your wife in the way you speak to her and in how you treat her generally. A man's prayers will be hindered if he dishonours and disrespects his wife. It is dishonourable to ignore your wife or walk out on her, when she is speaking to you.

You will not act that way to anyone you claim to honour. It is dishonourable to shout at your wife like a slave either privately or publicly. God commands you to honour your wife, there should be an attitude of great honour and respect in the way you speak to her.

Some man may say, *'my wife does not deserve to be respected because of her attitude.'*

The bible does not say you should respect and honour your wife when she behaves well. Honouring your wife is regardless of how she acts.

Your business is not to bother about how she acts, rather, focus on obeying God who commanded you to honour her. You will be amazed at the change that will happen in the life of your spouse once you start honouring her. This also applies to wives in their dealings with their husbands.

The message translation of the bible renders 1 Peter 3:7 interestingly, it says.

"The same goes for you husbands: Be good husbands to your wives. Honour them, delight in them. As women they lack some of your advantages. But in the new life of God's grace, you're equals. Treat your wives, then, as equals so your prayers don't run aground."

In the new life of God's grace God commands men to treat their wives as equals so that your prayers can be answered by God. Implying that God is watching and keeping a record of how you treat your wife before he answers your prayers. What is good for daddy is also good for mummy!

Husbands, love your wives, and be not bitter against them.

COLOSSIANS 3:19

God commands husbands to love their wives and not be bitter against them.

The Weymouth's Translation says, *"do not treat them harshly."* The message translation commands husbands not to take advantage of their wives.

A lot of men are guilty of treating their wives harshly. Your wife deserves to be respected and it should reflect in your words and actions towards her.

Are you a husband? Did you know that your prayers can go unanswered if you treat your wife with dishonour?

Honouring your wife causes your prayers to be answered. If you are facing difficulties now in your life and you need

God to answer you, I encourage you to go to your wife first and ask her to forgive you if you have been disrespecting and dishonouring her. Going forward, commit to deal with her in love, honour and respect, exactly the way God commanded you to and watch your home transformed into a haven of peace.

I proclaim peace and harmony upon every marriage today in Jesus name.

Salvation Prayer

Jesus died on the cross to provide a basis for God to cancel all your debts of sin as an act of God's love for you.

If you have not made the Lord Jesus Christ the Lord of you life and you would like to do so, then make these confessions.

Say; Heavenly Father, I believe that Jesus died for my sins. I believe that you God raise Him from the dead for my justification. Lord Jesus, I receive you into my heart as my lord and savior. I confess you today as Lord of my life. I am born again today in Jesus name.

About the Author

Emmanuel Ogbechie is the president of Divine Representatives Ministries Inc and Senior Pastor of Diplomats' Assembly Churches.

He is also the president of In His Presence Bible School with learning centres in several countries around the world.

He is the host of In His Presence Radio and TV broadcast.

A graduate of Electrical and Electronics Engineering, he is married to Pastor Idowu Ogbechie and they are blessed with a son Enoch.

To contact Pastor Emmanuel Ogbechie,

Please write or call

Divine Representatives Ministries,

P. O. Box 3631

Randburg 2125, Johannesburg,

South Africa

+27720809077

Or Visit online at

www.diplomatsassembly.org

If you have been blessed by this book, please include your testimonies and comments when you write.

OTHER BOOKS BY THE AUTHOR

PHYSICS OF MONEY

Money moves! Money was designed to move. It is either moving away from you or moving towards you.

Physics of money reveals the dynamics of the movement of money and shows you how you can harness the ever moving attribute of money.

If you desire financial freedom, the physics of Money is a must read. It is written in simple and concise language and will spur into action, so that you can move from where you are to where you desire to be financially. It is financial Intelligence expose at its best.

ISBN:

9781463502423

Sharing Intimacies With God

Developing a deeper life of prayer

The father is seeking for spirit worshippers, a generation of men and women who love to dwell In His Presence, just to share intimacies with Him.

Your prayer life is the key to transformation in every aspect of your life. As you deepen your prayer life and find reality in God's presence your whole life will be lifted into a glorious realm.

Pastor Emmanuel Ogbechie in this book **Sharing Intimacies with God** will inspire you to harness the amazing benefits of sharing intimacies with God through praying in the spirit.

A life of power is possible to those who discover Elijah's secret of prayer. Pastor Emmanuel Ogbechie in his characteristic style in this book will stir, energize and motivate you to rise and pray!

ISBN : 978-0-620-79172-4

TESTIMONIES ABOUT SHARING INTIMACIES WITH GOD BOOK

I got the book yesterday, got home and started reading it. I have finished reading it. This book is going to change my prayer life.

I encourage those who haven't bought it to get it. Your prayer life is the key to transformation in every aspect of your life.

Thank you daddy for this powerful book, Sharing Intimacies with God.

MP from Johannesburg

Reading Sharing Intimacies with God has changed my prayer life significantly and has drawn me closer to God. The relationship between me and God is stronger. Every time I read I end up praying in tongues involuntarily because of the powerful revelations in the book.

The chapters are nice and short which makes it easy to read, if you don't read the bible or are lazy to pray, it is the book for you. It is spirit filled.

If you are depressed or feel weak, read that book, it will encourage you to pray without ceasing easily.

Khodi, Capetown

HOW GRACE WORKS

A Revelation of the Dynamics of the Operation of Grace

by

Pastor Emmanuel Ogbechie

Everything God does in the New Testament He does it by Grace. God does everything He does by grace so that no one can glory in His sight that he obtained any height by his effort.

When Jesus walked the streets of Jerusalem, he lived to demonstrate to us how the grace of God works. If you do not know how grace works, you will not be able to experience its operation in your life as you desire.

In this book Pastor Emmanuel Ogbechie will help you discover HOW GRACE WORKS. You will learn about the operational procedure of the grace of God and this knowledge will catapult you to receive and experience a greater measure of the workings of God in your life.

The Law came by Moses but Jesus Christ brought the knowledge of Grace and how it works.

Pastor Emmanuel Ogbechie, host of In His Presence Radio and TV Broadcasts, is the founder and senior Pastor of Diplomats Assembly Churches also known as Divine Representatives Ministries Inc. He is the President of In His Presence Bible School and author of physics of money.

ISBN:

9780620791717

DEALING WITH ECONOMIC HARDSHIP

A Spiritual Response to Financial Difficulties!

God's plan for every Christians is financial abundance. He has also provided principles which when followed will yield the desired financial freedom.

Financial Hardship is real to many today! Satan has built a failing system upon the earth that God created for man's good and he is behind all forms of financial difficulty. To deal with financial hardship, it is important to put out a spiritual response.

Dealing with Economic Hardship will show you what God wants you to do in order to turn around your financial situation. You will discover the right spiritual response and learn how to overcome financial resistance.

Pastor Emmanuel Ogbechie will inspire you through biblical principles to respond to Financial Hardship and take your financial fortunes in your hands.

ISBN 978-0-6399569-0-9

FAITH THE SUBSTANCE OF THINGS

Understanding the principles of Faith

Faith is a spiritual substance. It is the substance of things hoped for. All things were created by God through the application of the principles of Faith. If you have faith and understand the dynamics of how faith works you can create anything you desire and find satisfaction to all your hearts desires.

Faith is all you need to please God. It will bring healing to your body and transform every aspect of your life. Faith is the best way of living because that is the way God lives. We have been called to live by the same faith of him who loved us and gave Himself for us.

ISBN - 978-0-6399569-2-3

THE OUTPOURING

Of the

HOLY SPIRIT

Experience the Spirit without measure

"And it shall come to pass afterward, that I will pour out my Spirit upon all flesh" The prophet Joel prophesied the outpouring of the Spirit many years ago and on the day of Pentecost after the Apostles spent many days praying in the upper room the promise prophesied began to be fulfilled. Peter declared on that day; "But [*instead*] this is [*the beginning of*] what was spoken through the prophet Joel:

The promise of the outpouring of the Holy Spirit is not time bound. From generation to generation when believers reach out to the father for a fresh outpouring the father always responds. If what happened on the day of Pentecost was the beginning then the glory of the latter house shall surpass the former.

You will be spurred to seek the manifestation of the spirit like you have never known before. ISBN - 97806399569-5-4

www.ingramcontent.com/pod-product-compliance
Lightning Source LLC
Chambersburg PA
CBHW031136090426
42738CB00008B/1104